COLLECTION OF DR. PHILIP BATCHELDER

Who's that in the globe?

The photographer.

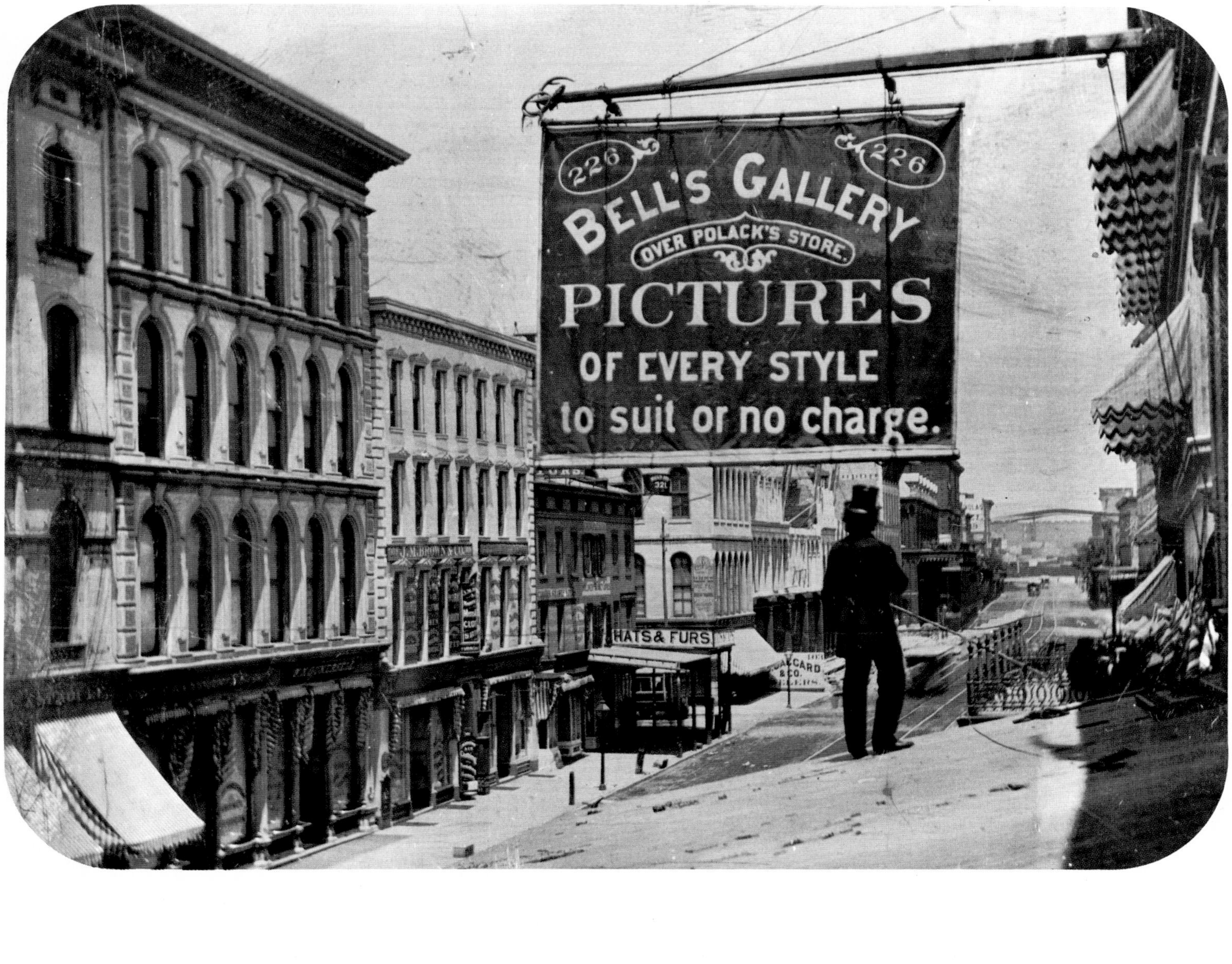

One flight up, he began recording history.

The miracle of reality caught every eye.

H. L. ELLIS
PHOTOGRAPHER

STATE HISTORICAL SOCIETY OF WISCONSIN

The horse, still king of the road, pulled his darkrooms everywhere.

He went up to take the growing city. He peered down deep into the depths.

LA ROCHE
VIEWS
1115

CHICAGO HISTORICAL SOCIETY

KANSAS STATE HISTORICAL SOCIETY

LIBRARY OF CONGRESS

LIBRARY OF CONGRESS

LOS ANGELES COUNTY MUSEUM

NEW HAVEN COLONY HISTORICAL SOCIETY

Very little in the life of the people,

BOTH: CULVER PICTURES

HAYNES STUDIOS INC.

NEW YORK STATE HISTORICAL ASSOCIATION

BROWN BROTHERS

CULVER PICTURES

UNIVERSITY OF KANSAS

or in their death, escaped his probing lens.

HISTORY OF PHOTOGRAPHY COLLECTION
SMITHSONIAN INSTITUTION

Oliver Jensen

Joan Paterson Kerr

Murray Belsky

American Album

Published by AMERICAN HERITAGE PUBLISHING CO., INC.

Book Trade Distribution by SIMON and SCHUSTER

STAFF FOR THIS BOOK

Oliver Jensen, *Writer*
Joan Paterson Kerr, *Picture Editor*
Murray Belsky, *Art Director*
Richard S. Glassman, *Associate Art Director*
Rosemary L. Klein, *Chief of Research*
Mary Dawn Earley, *Editorial Assistant*
Nancy S. Kaufman, *Editorial Assistant*
Anne Lunt, *Copy Editor*

The excerpt on page 309 is reprinted with permission of The Macmillan Company from the Autobiography of William Allen White, *copyright 1946 by The Macmillan Company. The poem on page 293 is "The Old Feminist," from* Times Three, *by Phyllis McGinley, copyright 1953 by Phyllis McGinley; originally appeared in* The New Yorker; *reprinted by permission of The Viking Press, Inc.*

The endpapers, both photographs by Alice Austen, show a pond near Concord, Massachusetts, at the front, and rag-pickers on a New York street, at the back. The pictures on the preceding pages present photographers at work in the early days, and are in general self-explanatory. The very first picture, on page 1, is of a glass globe on the lawn of the Fort William Henry Hotel at Lake George; in it the photographer finds himself reflected. The enormous camera which appears silhouetted on the title page belonged to George R. Lawrence, a specialist in complex photography (see Introduction). He built this fourteen-hundred-pound affair on order—to make a picture eight feet long of the crack train of the Chicago and Alton Railroad. The resulting photograph later won the "Grand Prize of the World" at the Paris Exposition in 1900—but only after the French consul in New York had been sent all the way to Chicago to see Lawrence's camera and make sure the elongated picture was not a fake.

ENDPAPERS: STATEN ISLAND HISTORICAL SOCIETY

 Library of Congress Catalogue Card Number: 68-29348

LIBRARY OF CONGRESS

Table of Contents

Introduction

To the authors of this book, a photograph is a kind of miracle, even in a world that has unlocked the atom and reached far out into the universe. And an old photograph, going back a century and more, is a still greater miracle. It is not just because these ancient and fragile daguerreotypes and glass plates are so surprisingly sharp and clear, despite the difficulties under which they were made, despite the primitive and bulky equipment. It is because these scenes long vanished and people long dead spring out at us as though it were yesterday; as though these rigidly posed ladies and gentlemen will rise in a moment to bow to each other and, perhaps, to us; as though the steamboat at the landing will presently whistle, pull in its gangplank, and steam majestically off.

A photograph is indeed the living past, as neither words nor art can ever be, however cunningly contrived. There before you, frozen forever, is the light that fell on a human face—someone you loved, or someone you never knew; an ancestor or a famous man, or someone quite unknown—but there he is, to the life: the odd hair, the unblinking eyes, the funny collar. The light that fell on that face reaches us a century later, bringing with it a precisely truthful image of what our eyes would have seen from the same vantage point, down to the last wrinkle.

It is the faithfulness to fact, at least to what appeared before the lens, that has made photography a great new tool for the historian, even if he sometimes fails to employ it. Hitherto he could describe; he had relics, records, ruins; he had art, although it was sparse and rarely literal. But after 1839, when photography burst upon the world, he could show things exactly as they were. Think what it would mean to have an entirely accurate likeness of Washington, to have photographs with Plutarch's *Lives,* or to see the Colossus of Rhodes as Herodotus did (what a magnet to photographers that would have been!).

It is true, of course, that most people who pose for their pictures are not thinking of history, and would never suppose they were part of it. And most photographers, whether professional or amateur, are simply recording likenesses, weddings, holidays, street scenes, picnics, back yards, front porches, Charlie in front of the Capitol, Sally squinting into the sun. Yet it is out of such ephemera, scattered in a million albums, attics, files, and shoe boxes, that we can reconstruct the ordinary life of another era. How did people dress and wear their hair? How did they enjoy themselves, and what were their jobs like? What was their idea of taste? This is social history, or the life of the anonymous multitudes, and it is just as important an element in understanding the past as the work of the journalistic photographer who follows the news and the famous people who make it. Few people think historically, and even fewer would bother to go out and preserve for posterity the countryside, the city, and the street with its buildings, its signs, its passersby, its parade of vehicles. Why photograph these mundane things? They will be the same tomorrow. No one thinks, as he glances idly about him, that what he sees may be greatly altered in a decade, and often unrecognizable in half a century. But it is so.

The purpose of this book is to revisit an utterly vanished earlier America by means of old photographs as fresh and revealing as we could find. In terms of time they run from 1839, when the first daguerreotypes were taken, until the eve of the First World War, which marks the end of an era, or what we may regard as the beginning of our own time.

We begin with our earliest pictures, and move on to show how the camera discovered one aspect of America after another, but our arrangement is not otherwise chronological. This is not a political or military history of the United States, and the few famous people in it appear for incidental reasons, like Walt Whitman with two little children, or Chief Justice Salmon P. Chase because he happens to be part of a fine tableau on someone's verandah. It should also be made clear that we have not prepared a book of famous photographs, or a history of photography. In our selection we have consciously slighted or excluded the work of many eminent men, from Morse and Brady through Stieglitz and Steichen. This policy does not imply any disrespect for great and famous pictures; but such pictures, being familiar, are the warp and woof of quite another tapestry than this one. We could not give a balanced portrait of the era without including some few photographs that have appeared before, but even then we have tried to avoid the best known and to present them in such size or detail that new dimensions appear. Many of our final choices have been printed in a size enlarged several times from their original; a photograph, mildly interesting in a small size, may become absolutely compelling when blown up. Then the faces leap out of the crowds. Signs become legible and one can make out the pictures on a wall, those perennial indicators of period and class.

Whenever we could find them, we have gone back to the original plates and negatives for fresh, sharp prints; imperfections linger, however, either because they were there to start with or because in the long passage of time many an old photograph has received rough treatment. We have not hesitated to crop some of the pictures, sometimes to remove a damaged portion but more often to heighten drama or interest. A few bad holes, where emulsion has peeled off old glass plates, have been grayed in to avoid distracting the eye, and modern dirt has been cleaned off. But we have been scrupulous not to retouch or to "highlight" pictures, and to leave the ancient scratches, cracks, and spots exactly as they were, for they have an honorable history.

It is almost mandatory, it seems, that an inventor be laughed at the moment he displays his brain child, but this, oddly enough, did not happen when Louis Jacques Mandé Daguerre, who was already known in Paris as a painter and exhibitor of lifelike dioramas, publicly announced in 1839 that he had succeeded in freezing on a plate an image obtained through a camera obscura. Perhaps the reason no one laughed was that the inventor had proof in his hand, exquisite and convincing proof, and also that he had taken the precaution of going to the right people first, and of taking his time.

Daguerre was partly an inventor, partly an impresario. The camera, which brought an inverted image through a pinhole or lens into a darkened room (literally, camera obscura), and later, a small box employing the same principle had been known to artists for centuries. Reflected onto a ground glass, the image could be traced, to save a painter much labor in sketching landscapes, buildings, and people. It was known to Leonardo, who described it in his notebooks; he once said, as if in reference to the device: "That painting is most praiseworthy which is most like the thing represented." Dürer knew about it, Canaletto and Bellotto and others used it. But the dream of many artists that they could in some magical way "fix" the image or make it permanent—that remained impossible, at least until the early nineteenth century, a brilliant era of discovery all over the world. The English scientist Sir John Herschel, his countryman William Henry Fox Talbot, and the American painter and inventor Samuel F. B. Morse were all experimenting with the fact that salts of silver will register differences in light and dark.

The first man to achieve any great success was a Frenchman named Nicéphore Niépce, during the 1820's. Through the medium of a Paris optician, who made lenses for both men, Daguerre met Niépce in 1826, and they formed a partnership in 1829. Exactly who did what first is lost in the mists of history, but it is known that Niépce made crude photographs in the 1820's, and Daguerre the first good ones in the 1830's. Niépce died in 1833, and Daguerre pushed on alone. One of his pictures survives from 1837. (Fox Talbot, who was working with paper and making negatives, actually produced photographs, or what he later called "calotypes" or "talbotypes," as early as 1835; but he did not publish until after Daguerre and his work, important later, had at the start very little effect.)

The process was scarcely simple. Daguerre had plated a sheet of copper with a thin coating of silver, which was then highly polished. This in turn he quickened, or activated, in a closed box over fumes of iodine, to make the silver sensitive to light; then, in darkness, he placed it in a plate holder which he slipped into a camera on a steady tripod. The exposure, which required from a quarter to half an hour, was an improvement over Niépce's eight hours, but it was adapted only to subjects that did not move. Daguerre had attempted no portraits. When his process was completed, nothing was visible on the silver plate. Ralph Waldo Emerson, brooding over this piece of information, was moved to comment: "The strangeness of the discovery is that Daguerre should have known that a picture was there when he could not see any. When the plate is taken from the camera, it appears just as when it was put there, spotless silver; it is then laid over steam-

THE HISTORICAL SOCIETY OF PENNSYLVANIA

The earliest surviving daguerreotype in America, taken by Joseph Saxton in 1839; reproduced in the exact size of the original

MRS. JOSEPH CARSON

Probably the earliest surviving photograph of a face: Robert Cornelius, taken by himself

SMITHSONIAN INSTITUTION

Another claimant as first: this self-portrait by Henry Fitz, Jr., who had to keep his eyes closed

BROWN BROTHERS

Long believed the earliest portrait, but actually not; Miss Draper, photographed in 1840

ing mercury and the picture comes out." Strange indeed; even to modern minds.

After the mercury treatment, the plate was submerged in a solution of sodium hyposulphite (the "hypo" of modern times, discovered by Herschel and quickly adopted by Daguerre). These salts arrested the action of the other chemicals and fixed the image permanently. After a washing to get rid of the hypo, the completed daguerreotype, so delicate it could be marred by a touch, was placed under glass in a case. The result was a positive, a one-of-a-kind picture that could be duplicated only by taking another daguerreotype of it. It could not be viewed in every light, but had to be turned a little to bring out the image.

For all its drawbacks, however, Daguerre's was a thrilling discovery. When it was announced, on August 19, 1839, before the French academies of sciences and of fine arts, it was quickly published all over Europe. In an age like our own, when the fact of photography is commonplace, when we make pictures move, and transmit them through the air, and even send them from the moon, it is hard to grasp the excitement with which the writers, thinkers, and artists of the period received Daguerre's discovery. The editor of a New York magazine, *The Knickerbocker,* wrote the same year: "We have seen the views taken in Paris by the 'Daguerreotype' and have no hesitation in avowing that they are the most remarkable objects of curiosity and admiration, in the arts, that we ever beheld. Their exquisite perfection almost transcends the bounds of sober belief. Let us endeavor to convey to the reader an impression of their character. Let him suppose himself standing in the middle of Broadway, with a looking glass held perpendicularly in his hand, in which is reflected the street, with all that therein is, for two or three miles, taking in the haziest distance. Then let him take the glass into the house, and find the impression of the entire view, in the softest light and shade, vividly retained upon its surface. This is the Daguerreotype! . . . There is not an object even in the most minute, embraced in that wide scope, which was not in the original; and it is impossible that one should have been omitted. Think of that!"

"The mirror with a memory," Oliver Wendell Holmes called it, and the French artist Paul Delaroche spoke for many when he exclaimed, "From today painting is dead!" (There was a reply of sorts from the noted American landscapist Thomas Cole: "If you believe everything the newspapers say . . . you would be led to suppose that the poor craft of painting was knocked in the head by this new machinery for making Nature take her own likeness, and we nothing to do but give up the ghost. . . . But the art of painting is creative, as well as an imitative art, and is in no danger of being superseded by any mechanical contrivance.")

News of the daguerreotype reached America on September 20, 1839, on board the steamer *British Queen.* Within a few weeks there were tinkering American artists and inventors in every city busily attempting, with varying results, to imitate Daguerre. But in America the true father of the new device was Samuel Morse, who had a head start of many months over the others. He had been in Paris in early 1839, trying to obtain a French patent for his electromagnetic telegraph, and on March 7 of that year he had called on Daguerre, who showed his visitor some photographs without disclosing his method. "The exquisite minuteness of the delineation cannot be conceived," Morse wrote in a letter home. "No painting or engraving ever approached it. . . . The impressions of interior views are Rembrandt perfected." One flaw in the process he had immediately noticed: "Objects moving are not impressed. The Boulevard, so constantly filled with a moving throng of pedestrians and carriages, was perfectly solitary, except an individual who was having his boots brushed. His feet were compelled, of course, to be stationary for some time, one being on the box of the boot black, and the other on the ground. Consequently his boots and legs were well defined, but he is without body or head, because these were in motion."

Within eight days of receiving the news that came on the *British Queen* Morse was exhibiting a view—now lost—of the New York Unitarian Church, taken from a window of New York University, where he was teaching at the time. Taking a partner, John W. Draper, professor of chemistry, Morse began to experiment with the idea of making portraits; he posed his daughter and some of her friends, motionless and eyes closed, for ten- and twenty-minute periods in the sunlight on a college roof. These photographs too, it seems, have been lost. Draper, who had already been working with lenses, light, and light-sensitive materials before

Daguerre's announcement, decided that by increasing the aperture and shortening the focal length he could bring a stronger image to bear on his silver plate. He also substituted chlorine for iodine in sensitizing it, which reduced the exposure time. At first he dusted his subjects' faces with flour to whiten them, and had them close their eyes. None of the results are known to exist today, but we do possess what is often erroneously called the first photographic portrait in America, a fine daguerreotype he took in the first half of 1840 of his handsome sister, Dorothy Catherine Draper (page 16). She sat under strong reflected light for sixty-five seconds. Draper proudly sent the daguerreotype to Herschel in England, where it survived for almost a century; finally it was destroyed when someone tried to clean it.

The whole question of "firsts" in the early days of American photography is difficult. There are a number of rival claimants working within days and weeks of each other. So much work is lost, or badly dated, that most assertions must be hedged. The earliest known surviving American photograph is the little picture on page 15, which we reproduce in its exact original size of 4.5 by 5.9 centimeters. This fuzzy and scarcely artistic view was taken from a window of the U.S. Mint in Philadelphia, and it shows the Pennsylvania Arsenal and the cupola of Central High School. The man who took it, Joseph Saxton, was a skilled mechanic at the mint who had read about Daguerre's new process in a local paper. Improvising a camera from an old "seegar box," as he called it, and an ordinary burning or magnifying glass, and using a piece of the silver ribbon from which coins used to be stamped, he took this picture with a long exposure on October 16, 1839.

As to portraits, most of the very first have not survived. Among those still in existence, a leading contender to the title of "earliest" is a self-portrait (page 16) of Robert Cornelius, a Philadelphia lampmaker and skilled artisan with metals. He had seen Saxton's view and set about making his own equipment. "I was alone and ran in front of the camera," he recalled thirty years later, giving many details but no exact date. Another claimant was Henry Fitz, Jr., a New York telescope maker who photographed himself, his eyes closed to prevent blurring, in late 1839 or early 1840 (page 16).

For a brief time, photography was a small club. Morse, hard up at the time and eking out his professor's salary, began training daguerreotypists, among them a farm boy from upstate New York named Mathew B. Brady, a young civil engineer named Edward Anthony, who was having trouble finding work in his field, and a young Boston man named Albert S. Southworth, who later founded the noted firm of Southworth and Hawes. Presently Morse turned back to his inventions, and to politics; his students went on to create an industry.

It was inevitable that, once launched into the field, the daguerreotypists should seek to branch out. One of the first was Anthony, who went to Washington in 1843 and with a partner set about taking the likenesses of all the members of Congress and other important figures. It was an ambitious undertaking but an agreeable one; Thomas Hart Benton, chairman of the Senate Military Affairs Committee, accommodatingly turned over his committee room to Anthony for a studio. The great collection that resulted was widely exhibited until destroyed by a fire in 1852, a disaster for history from which only a famous picture of old John Quincy Adams is definitely known to survive. Since more than one daguerreotype was taken at a sitting, however, a good many other Anthony pictures, probably including the portrait on page 29 of Lewis Cass, Democratic candidate for President in 1848, may be part of a collection of great men of the era now preserved at the Chicago Historical Society.

One often wishes that early photographers had taken more care in recording facts and dates on the backs of daguerreotypes. Because so much is open to speculation, a great deal of detective work is required. The earliest known photograph of Abraham Lincoln, which appears on page 19 together with a companion picture of his wife, is a case in point. Research by Frederick Hill Meserve and by Lloyd Ostendorf now attributes these haunting daguerreotypes to N. H. Shepherd of Springfield, Illinois. A servant of the Lincolns recalled that Mrs. Lincoln later said of them that they were "very precious to me, taken when we were very young and so desperately in love. They will grace the walls of the White House." Lincoln is supposed to have commented, "I trust that grace never slips a peg and becomes dis-grace."

AMERICAN MUSEUM OF PHOTOGRAPHY

The first aerial photograph: a view of Boston, taken from a balloon by J. W. Black in 1860

BEINECKE LIBRARY, YALE UNIVERSITY

One of the first war photographs: a daguerreotype of General Wool and his staff at Saltillo, Mexico

POLK ANCESTRAL HOME

President James K. Polk and his wife Sarah, a daguerreotype of 1849

While some of the "professors" behind the lenses maintained that they were carefully searching out the character and hidden qualities of their subjects, there was no attempt at modern "glamour," as must be apparent from the plain and gloomy double portrait, possibly by Brady, reproduced on this page of President and Mrs. James K. Polk on Valentine's Day, 1849, just before they left the White House and only a few months before he died.

Once embarked, of course, the camera moved in all directions. President Polk's war with Mexico, for example, was captured in a set of dim daguerreotypes made by some enterprising but unknown hand in 1846 and 1847 and found some years later in an attic in Yonkers, New York. A little one appears on page 17, freezing General Wool and his staff at Saltillo, Mexico. Photographers—Edward Anthony among them—were making pictures of the frontier; others, like the celebrated Langenheim brothers of Philadelphia, were photographing the country and its natural wonders, to be reproduced in endless sets of slides for the home stereopticon. They abandoned the daguerreotype and bought rights to Fox Talbot's patented calotype method, with its advantage of furnishing a negative from which thousands of prints could be made. In Boston one truly ambitious man, James Wallace Black (who also took the picture on pages 204–205), succeeded after several abortive attempts in making the first American aerial photographs, in a balloon held captive by a cable over Boston Common in October, 1860. When Oliver Wendell Holmes saw the pictures, one of which appears on page 17, he was moved to describe them as "Boston as the eagle and the wild goose see it."

Black was naturally using the new photographic method, the so-called "wet plate," which produced a negative on glass. It was a cumbersome method, as we point out later in this book, but it had the great advantage of producing as many prints as one wanted. In addition, the sensitive wet plate gave excellent quality with only a few seconds' exposure if the subject was in the sun. Introduced in 1851, wet plates made possible the publishing of photographs for use in the home stereopticon, but they did not supersede the daguerreotype (and its short-lived successor, the ambrotype) until ten years later.

With the wet plate, then, paper photographic prints appeared and proliferated, particularly in the form of little mounted prints called *cartes de visite,* which were indeed often used as calling cards. And photography speeded up. Later, with the invention of the dry plate, then the hand-held camera, and finally George Eastman's Kodak (with its flexible film) in 1888, photography gradually achieved what is called "instantaneous exposure"; yet some photographers, including many of the best, kept alive older methods side by side with the new.

More than two hundred of the pictures in this book where taken by, or are attributed to, known photographers, and the remainder are anonymous. In certain cases, such as the pictures taken by the Byron Company, we cannot be sure which individual members of a photographic partnership were responsible, nor is categorization of our diverse findings always easy. The difference, for example, between professional and amateur tends to blur in many cases. A few of the photographers were specialists—men like Darius Kinsey, with his concentration on loggers; Edward S. Curtis, with his extensive coverage of Indians; and George Collins Cox, the notable New York portraitist. Such a grouping would also include George R. Lawrence, an Illinois farm boy with a gift for drawing and inventing who became one of the world's most noted photographers around the turn of the century. Lawrence, who built the high-tripod device on page 8 and the immense camera on our title page, also invented a flashlight powder which was in standard use until the development of flash bulbs. As "Flashlight Lawrence," he first made possible the photography of indoor events like conventions and banquets. Turning to aerial photography, he experimented successfully with high poles, collapsible towers, and camera-carrying kites (controlled electrically from the ground); such equipment got him into the business of making bird's-eye pictures like that of the balloon meet on pages 148–149.

The frontier photographers, men like William Henry Jackson, F. Jay Haynes, and others described in our second and third chapters, were wanderers and adventurers. Some who wandered to a different drum were the photographers with social consciences—Lewis Hine, concerned with labor and the poor; Alexander Gardner, determined to show the true colors of war and rebellion; and Frances

Benjamin Johnston, a talented, well-educated woman who made herself into what would be called today a "feature" photographer. She chronicled life aboard Admiral Dewey's flagship, the *Olympia,* in 1899, and from the Harrison administration through that of Taft she took many of the best-known White House people and events. But her heart was really in what used to be known as "the uplift," that is, the possibility of reforming an always imperfect society, and she became known for her powerful pictures of life in the harsh coal fields of Pennsylvania and of students at Hampton Institute and Tuskegee.

Two other able women, close contemporaries of Miss Johnston, are represented by many pictures in this book, and, while the camera has no sex, it has enough special talents in a woman's hands to make another category for us. Alice Austen, a well-born maiden lady of Staten Island, New York, was concerned not with uplift but with the ordinary life and activities of her friends and neighbors. She filled box after box with carefully annotated glass plates of unrivalled social history—houses, cluttered interiors, jolly Victorian parties, carriages, sports, summer travels. Branching out, she took pictures of Eastern cities, of the waterfront (see her fine picture on pages 130—131), and of the street "types" who give a place its flavor. Wiped out by the Depression, she wound up on the Staten Island poor farm, and was only rescued as a very old lady when her vast collection of plates was rediscovered and published for her benefit.

The third notable yet forgotten lady photographer was Chansonetta Stanley Emmons of Kingfield, Maine, who was born in 1858. She turned to photography as a solace when her husband, James Nathaniel Emmons, died only ten years after their marriage. It was a wise choice, since she had not only a fine sense of lighting and composition but also a steady source of plates; her twin brothers, F. E. and F. O. Stanley, had invented and were manufacturing a dry plate. Later on, they devised a still more remarkable and famous invention, the Stanley Steamer automobile. Like Miss Austen, Mrs. Emmons was a gently reared lady with a good eye and inexhaustible interest in her surroundings, and she set out to preserve on glass the old-fashioned sights of Maine—the blacksmith, the farms, the kitchens, the children. It was a simple yet unforgettable achievement.

The ideal source for a book of this kind is indeed someone like Mrs. Emmons, the photographer who spends a lifetime in one town or city and records what happens there. Gradually, perhaps without meaning to, such a photographer becomes a local institution and over the years accumulates a kind of history of his area. Very occasionally he becomes famous for it, like Arnold Genthe, a San Francisco portraitist whose great artistry in photographing the local Chinatown is still celebrated, or the Byrons, who covered New York. But more often the local photographer toils along with only fleeting local fame: Henry Hamilton Bennett in the Wisconsin Dells; Theodore Teeple of Wooster and Massillon, Ohio; Belle Johnson, who labored fifty-five years in little Monroe, Missouri; the Howes brothers of Ashfield, Massachusetts; Joseph J. Pennell, who left behind him thirty thousand negatives—several tons of glass—recording almost more than anyone would care to know about the life of Junction City, Kansas, and nearby Fort Riley; W. A. Raymond, who travelled widely in the early days of Oregon state making a record of one of the last frontiers.

It is not important to pick a large, busy place. Raymond, for example, concentrated on bleak little Moro, Oregon, and Henry Madison Wantland picked Stillwater, Oklahoma. The point is to stick to it over a long time, and to love it. This was superlatively true of Arthur J. Telfer, who succeeded Washington G. Smith as the foremost photographer of Cooperstown, New York. The combined output of the firm, which was in business for a century, totals some sixty thousand negatives, nearly all on glass; it is rare that such a record exists without total or partial destruction, even rarer that it is adequately captioned. It was also true of Charles J. Van Schaick, who did much the same as Telfer for little Black River Falls, Wisconsin; according to the local historical society, which has had to heft them, Van Schaick produced some two and a quarter tons of negatives in the years between 1880 and 1929. He took the farms, the good crops, the new thresher, little Winnebago Indian children leaving the reservation for the white man's school, all the quick and even the dead of the town where he became a local fixture, remembered to this day. It is with a selection of such material that we hope this book may make some contribution to American photographic history.

BOTH: LIBRARY OF CONGRESS

Congressman-elect Abe Lincoln in 1846, attributed to N. H. Shepherd

The new Congressman's bride, Mary Todd Lincoln, taken at the same time

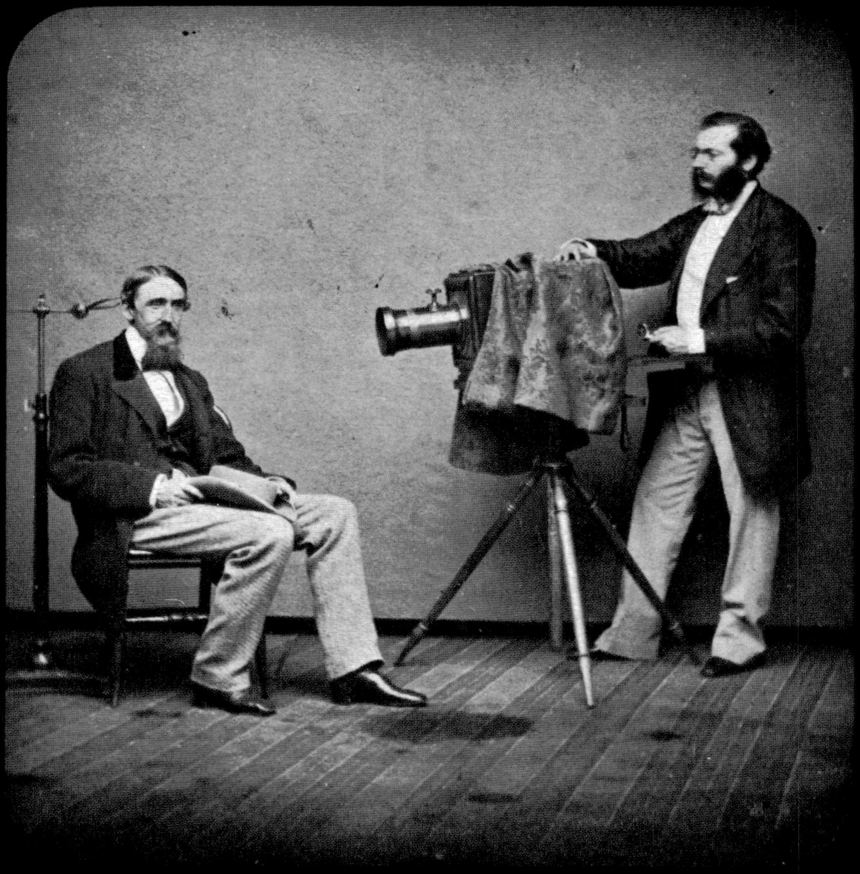

When Nothing Moved

The first great era in American photography is the time of the daguerreotype, running from the announcement of Daguerre's invention in 1839 to the verge of the Civil War, when it was displaced by the wet plate. The idea spread like wildfire. Suddenly there were "Daguerrian artists" and galleries everywhere —about one thousand advertised professionals by the end of the first decade and over three thousand by 1860, recording the strange, motionless world shown in this chapter. About three million of these "sun-drawn miniatures" were being made each year, the New York *Tribune* estimated in 1853. Some were works of art, and some were very poor. For the first time, however, anyone could have his portrait taken for a modest price.

Further proof that this was a democratic art was the fact that almost anyone could, and did, go into it. James F. Ryder, a well-known Cleveland photographer who remembered the early days, described them like this: "It was no uncommon thing to find watch repairers, dentists, and other styles of business folk to carry on daguerreotypy 'on the side'! I have known blacksmiths and cobblers to double up with it, so it was possible to have a horse shod, your boots tapped, a tooth pulled, or a likeness taken by the same man." Wherever they went, the itinerant photographers were welcomed by people longing for immortality. Here is an advertisement of the 1854 era: "The Subscriber having located his SALOON [sic] IN THIS VILLAGE for a short time would take this opportunity to inform the inhabitants . . . that he is now prepared to take ORIGINAL DAGUERREOTYPES. CASES, Every Description Furnished. Having devoted some time to the business, and being prepared with a good Apparatus, he feels confident in assuring the public that all Pictures taken by him shall give entire satisfaction. All who wish to obtain a GOOD LIKENESS, will remember to call at his SALOON without delay, as his stay in the village will be limited. J. A. FOSTER."

It was an experience no one forgot very quickly. You were plunked down on a chair or stood against an "artistic" backdrop, ladies demure, men confident, with a hand, perhaps, thrust into the tightly buttoned coat. A head clamp on a stand (see the picture at left) grasped you firmly from the back, to prevent motion, and you arranged an expression (usually stern) which you thought you could hold immobile for the minute or more required. The sunlight streamed on you, from a skylight or arrangement of mirrors. Here is how it affected the famous New York diarist George Templeton Strong, who had himself taken in 1842, at the age of twenty-two: "December 29. Had myself Daguerreotyped this morning.... It's a great bore—one doesn't know till he has tried how hard it is to sit without moving a muscle for two minutes.... The portrait of a man staring intently into vacancy and striving desperately to keep still must be unlike his usual appearance." To say the least! Yet some people were pleased indeed, as attested in this letter from a parent to a daguerreotypist, written in 1856: "It was only yesterday that I had the great pleasure of seeing the speaking daguerreotype of my little daughter. With two great difficulties to overcome in a child's want of repose and *this* child's changeful expression, you have made a portrait faithful as respects the resemblance... and charming as a work of art."

The great name from the era, of course, is Mathew Brady's, although he was not so much an "artist" as a straightforward reporter of the scenes and persons he encountered. He was in fact less a photographer than a businessman and the organizer of the work of others, men like Alexander Gardner, whom he brought over from Scotland, and Timothy O'Sullivan; both men are noted for their coverage of the Civil War. While still in his early twenties, Brady opened his own studio at the corner of Broadway and Fulton Street; there was plenty of competition from some seventy other galleries, but Brady had the biggest, and the most successful. He had ten operators ready to take your picture, and there was always an exhibition in the elegant rooms to draw in the curious, who came to gape and stayed to be photographed. Distinguished persons from every walk of life were captured by his cameras, including every President from John Quincy Adams to William McKinley, saving only William Henry Harrison, who died within a month of taking office. One picture that Brady carefully made himself in 1860 became a campaign instrument for Abraham Lincoln, who said later: "Brady and the Cooper Union speech made me President of the United States."

ALL: H. LAWRENCE HOFFMAN

This picture of an unknown mother and child, exquisite for all its flecks and imperfections, dates back to the heyday of the daguerreotype, in the early 1850's. We have enlarged it about four times the original size. The boy and his toy horse above are taken from an ambrotype, the kind of photograph on glass that began to replace the daguerreotype in the late 1850's. The daguerreotype, made on a copper plate coated with thin silver, was a positive, the ambrotype a glass negative that was made to look like a positive by covering the back with dark cloth, paint, or paper. At right we have a sad-faced little girl and her posy of flowers, photographed about the same time as the little boy above by Spooner Brothers, in a place unknown. The picture is an ambrotype which pays due tribute to "Cutting's Patent." James A. Cutting of Boston patented the short-lived ambrotype process in July, 1854.

BOTH: H. LAWRENCE HOFFMAN

Beauty, whether plain or exotic, sometimes stares hauntingly out of the quaint old portrait cases of the 1850's. You sat very still and sombre and seconds ticked slowly by until the "professor" (an ambrotypist in these cases) closed his lens. Both girls are unknown.

BOTH: H. LAWRENCE HOFFMAN

The male of the species was no less willing to pose, and less inhibited. This gentleman in a daguerreotype of the 1840's clutches a carnation in his teeth, for what reason we have not the slightest notion.

Ten years later, styles have changed, and another dandy is ambrotyped while biting a cigar. "Clothes make the man," observed Mark Twain. "Naked people have little or no influence in society."

PRIVATE COLLECTION

Out of this clear and hitherto unpublished daguerreotype comes the steady, commanding gaze of Frederick Douglass, the escaped slave who became the first true leader of his race in America. Once a field hand and house servant, he rose to be a noted orator who knew and advised great men of his time.

Here is the magnificent likeness of a fine old Roman, probably taken around 1851 by Edward Anthony, as one of a series on statesmen. Lewis Cass, a soldier of 1812, a senator, and Democratic candidate for President in 1848, was thinking of running again in 1852. Imagine him on a button!

BOTH: H. LAWRENCE HOFFMAN

It was less usual, but early America did not always pose in its Sunday best. Here, preserved in ambrotype, is a blacksmith with the tools of his trade, stiffly pretending he is about to shoe a horse. The year was about 1857 or 1858, and beards were slowly reappearing.

It was just as hard work to clean house as it was to make the anvil ring, although one was rarely photographed at it. Who this woman was we do not know, but she was prevailed upon to pose with apron, broom, and authoritative-looking keys, and she appears content.

Tools of one's trade? It depends on the line one takes up. This dangerous-looking chap, whose name, alas, is lost, was photographed about 1845 by an unknown hand. The snappy costume indicates a gentleman, at least of sorts, and the weapon (probably a Dragoon Colt) suggests that he was proud of his profession, on whatever side of the law it fell.

MINNESOTA HISTORICAL SOCIETY

This daguerreotype of a man posing with the tools of a gold miner—plus an optimistically labelled bag and a jug of strong waters—shows a colorful Minnesota frontiersman named George W. Northrup, a fur trader, Army scout, and mission schoolteacher for the Assiniboin Indians. Ironically, he was killed by Indian arrows in 1864, at the age of 27.

SUTTER'S FORT STATE HISTORICAL MONUMENT

The twins on a tintype are Uranie and Susanie Hutchinson. Clearly they are wearing their finest black frocks, but whether for mourning or in a more festive spirit would be difficult to say. It is equally clear that neither of them has a tooth in her head.

This striking portrait is an ambrotype of a Quaker gentleman, name unknown, from New Bedford, Massachusetts. His garb is already antique for the era of the picture, the late 1850's. He is stalwartly ignoring the photographer's classic "prop."

MAINE HISTORICAL SOCIETY

The group photograph came later, of course, than the single portrait, mainly because it multiplied the chances that someone would move and spoil the plate. That is what the baby has done in the daguerreotype at left, despite his mother's best efforts. She is Mrs. Kiah Sewall, and the four other children have held their poses admirably. The rather raffish group below comes down the years with some precise information, as happens so much less often than we would like. It is inscribed: "To Col. J. C. Frémont from four of the old California Battalion, August 29, 1848, Washington, D. C.," which indicates that these four romantic characters must have been with Frémont ("the Pathmarker of the West," as Allan Nevins calls him) in the famous march to Monterey, in July of 1846, and at the capture of Los Angeles in August.

LOS ANGELES COUNTY MUSEUM OF NATURAL HISTORY

BOTH: AMERICAN HERITAGE COLLECTION

Professor Henry Wadsworth Longfellow appears on the porch of his Cambridge home, Craigie House, in 1856. The poet was 49. Famous literary men were included in the 30 Portraits of Distinguished Americans, a set of glass slides by Frederick and William Langenheim of Philadelphia.

Washington Irving was 73 and sat basking in the sun at the door of his "little old-fashioned stone mansion," Sunnyside, at Irvington, New York, when Frederick Langenheim took this stereo slide in 1856. The fine old storyteller was writing his last great work, his Life of George Washington.

From the earliest days, Niagara Falls drew honeymooners and photographers alike. Posing at the Falls was so popular that many photographers used painted backdrops, good in all weather. Is this old ambrotype faked? It's almost impossible to say.
COLLECTION TIME-OUT ANTIQUES

MAINE HISTORICAL SOCIETY

The hardest thing to capture, in the era of the daguerreotype, was a street scene, because people and vehicles move, but Marcus Ormsbee of Portland, Maine, did very well with this view of Engine

Company Casco No. 1 at a fire on Middle Street in 1848. Every building shown here, all the shops and printing offices, even the grand Exchange with its dome, burned down in 19th-century fires.

THE RHODE ISLAND HISTORICAL SOCIETY

Old James Bucklin, a scion of Rhode Island, poses with his wife and three of their five grown-up children on the porch of his handsome Providence home. The whole neighborhood is industrial now.

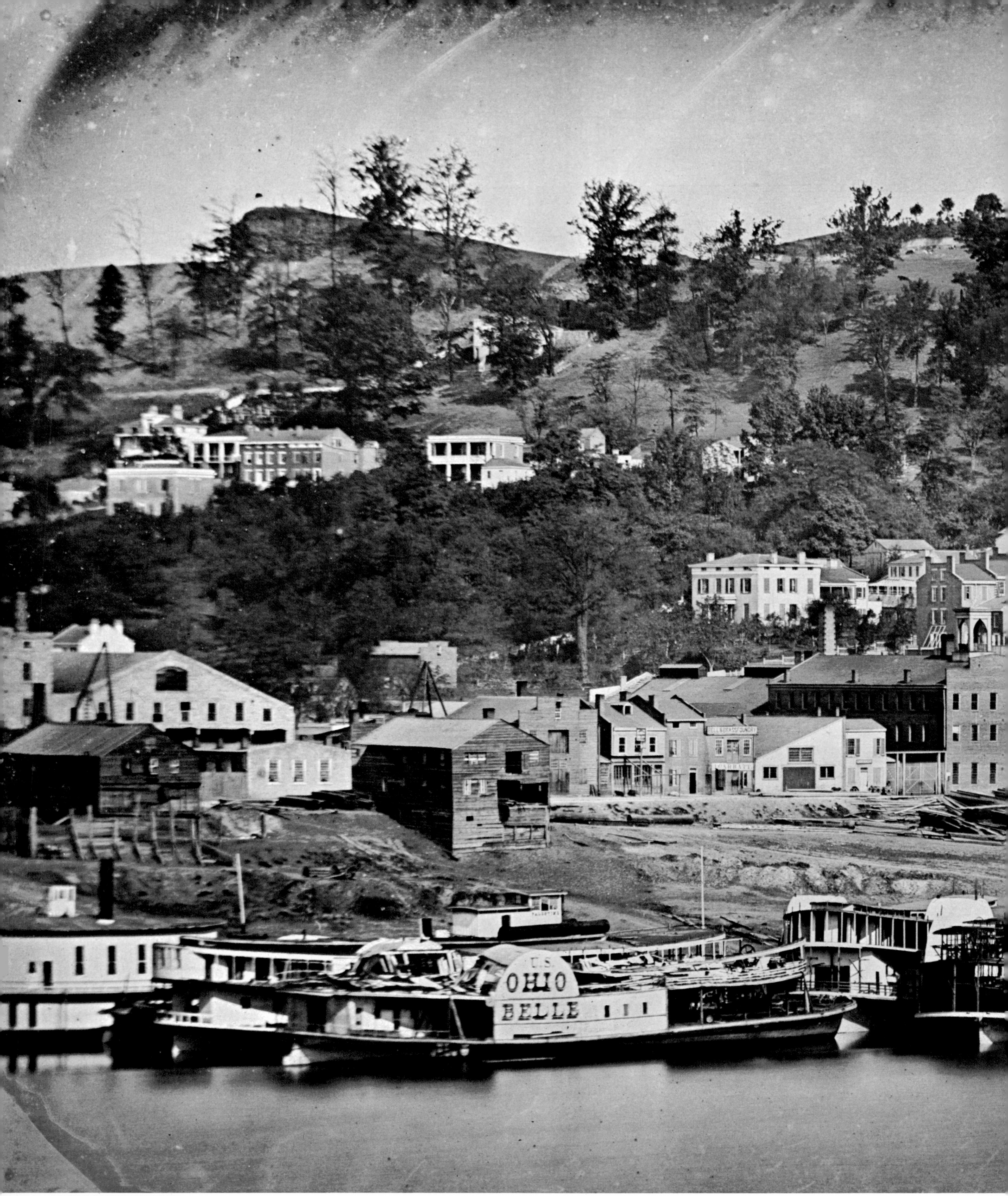

CINCINNATI PUBLIC LIBRARY

This remarkable early daguerreotype, thought to be the first to show a steamboat, is one of an eight-part panorama of the Cincinnati waterfront, taken from the Kentucky side of the Ohio River in 1848 by Charles Fontayne and William Southgate Porter. Above the steamboats, some of them

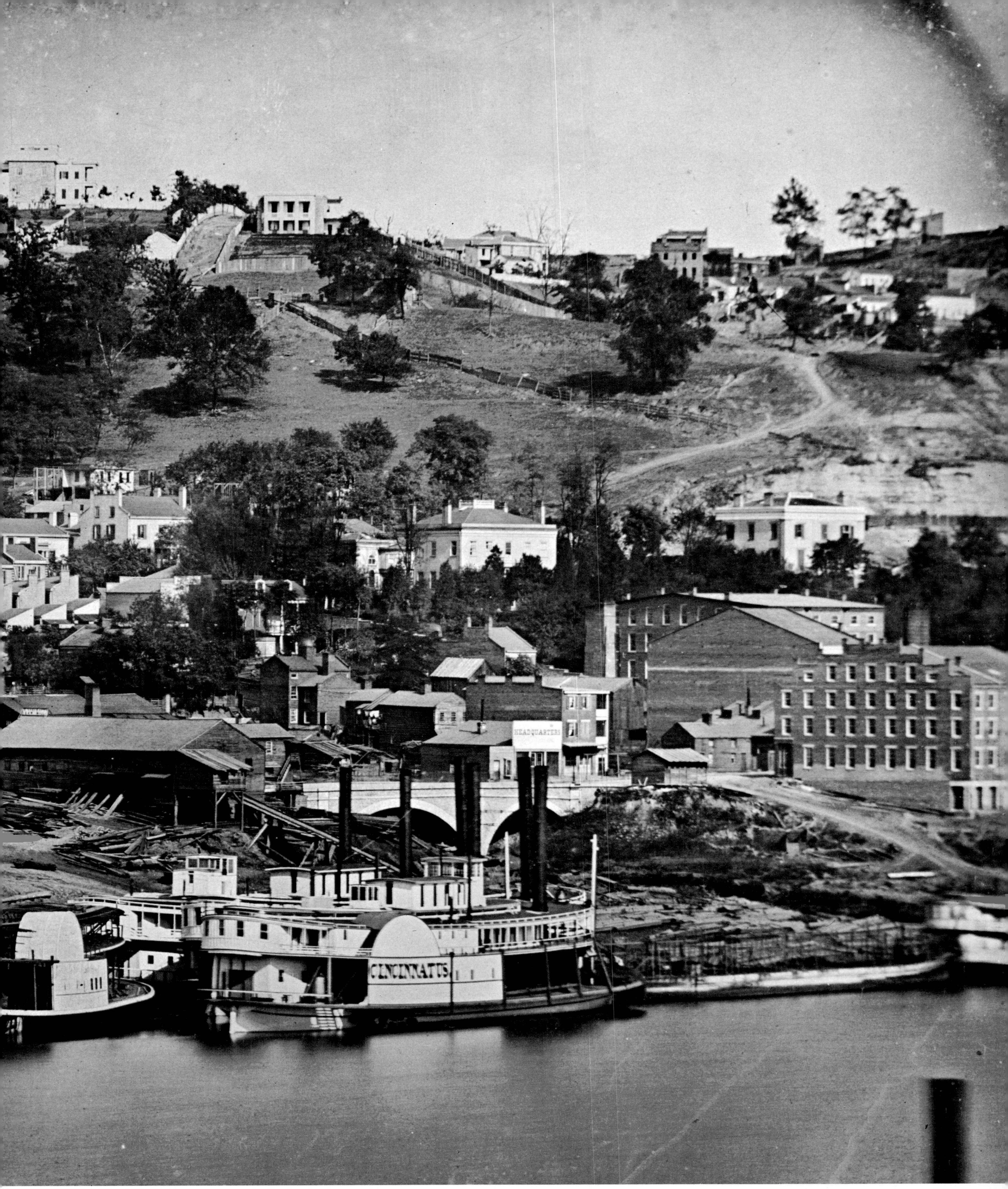

being dismantled, is a motley of buildings that have almost all vanished today. At the top of the hill, center, is an observatory that former President John Quincy Adams dedicated in 1843; it is gone today, and a large railroad, foot, and traffic bridge crosses the river in the center of this view.

COLLECTION OF JOSEPHINE COBB

Back in Washington, late in 1860, the Capitol was taking on recognizable form. The dome, under construction here, was completed in 1863; today's Mall was an untidy mess around a drainage canal. James Buchanan was President, Lincoln was newly elected, and the Union was falling apart.

Marcus Stevens & Co.
ROOMS.
FURNITURE WARE HOUSE.
J.S.JENNESS
LAMPS.
TEAS
GROCERIES.
H.R.ANDREWS
RAIL-ROAD HOTEL.
GENERAL STAGE OFFICE.
RAIL ROAD HOTEL

BURTON COLLECTION, DETROIT PUBLIC LIBRARY

A month after South Carolina demanded the surrender of Fort Sumter, the North was giving its answer in the manner shown in these two photographs. At left, the First Michigan, a "three-month regiment" raised in answer to Lincoln's call, musters on May 11, 1861, in a public square at Detroit before taking the cars for Washington. These men soon saw action, in the defeat at Bull Run in July, and that was the end of three-month regiments and notions about a short, easy war. Below, in the traditional manner of women in wartime, Philadelphia belles sew a battleflag for their men in one of the crowded exhibit rooms of the Pennsylvania Academy of Fine Arts. Observe that these are photographs, that is, paper prints from glass negatives made by the collodion "wet-plate" method, which came in on the verge of the Civil War and was used by Mathew Brady, Alexander Gardner, Timothy O'Sullivan and the other great war photographers. The war is not only a watershed in American history, dividing the modern industrial nation from the loosely federated young republic; it is also a landmark in the development of photographic techniques. The short-lived day of the stiffly posed, formal daguerreotype was over; the probing, inquisitive, reportorial photographer was at hand.

COLLECTION OF LLOYD OSTENDORF

BOTH: LIBRARY OF CONGRESS

Wars are fought by individuals, no matter how the histories are written. Here are three very raffish Confederate prisoners taken at Gettysburg and photographed by an unknown hand. How they contrast with the men at right! These three officers of the First Connecticut Artillery look much better turned out and better organized, as they pose for a photographer at Fort Brady on the James River. You know, somehow, that their side will win.

OVERLEAF: *The dreadful harvest of war is gathered by a burial party at Cold Harbor, Virginia, in this memorable picture made by J. Reekie and A. Gardner in April, 1865, ten months after these Union soldiers were killed. Men were often left unburied, or half-buried, during an angry war; but they did not die in vain, for the slaughter in June, 1864, inflicted punishment on Lee's Army of Northern Virginia from which the Confederacy never recovered.*

AMERICAN HERITAGE COLLECTION

AMERICAN HERITAGE COLLECTION

When the captains and the kings depart, we may expect the orators. Here they are on June 11, 1865, dedicating a monument on the battlefield of Bull Run (where the First Michigan, seen on pages 50-51, learned what war was about). Here, too, many dead lay unburied for months, but things

had been cleaned up a little for the services, hymns, parade, and four speeches. The sandstone monument still stands despite some vandalism, but the shells at the base are alive and have recently been removed in order to be deactivated. The picture was taken by W. Morris Smith and A. Gardner.

Opening the West

America had glimpsed the West before the Civil War, and when that agonizing struggle was over she turned vast energies loose upon it. Ex-soldiers of both sides thronged to the frontier, and through the summer months long caravans of covered wagons carried pioneers up along the Missouri and through the Rockies at South Pass. Where "The States" ended beyond the Mississippi a great host of colorful characters took over—grizzled guides and Indian scouts, old mountain trappers, bad men, prospectors, claim jumpers, faro dealers, pony express riders, women of uncertain virtue. Among them every now and then were the government survey parties, led by brilliant explorers like Clarence King, Ferdinand Vandeveer Hayden, John Wesley Powell, and George Wheeler, busy mapping all these new territories. Straight through the center of the great empty spaces the Union Pacific and the Western Pacific raced to a meeting of rails, which occurred at Promontory, Utah, in 1869. It was an exciting time and place to be alive—and we can see it plain, as it really was, in the work of pioneer photographers.

When that avid reporter and very modern man, Horace Greeley, made his way overland to California, he could not resist the language of the new art of photography in sketching there what he called "a rough ambrotype of life." But the new way of recording the actuality of things soon progressed beyond the ambrotype. During the Civil War photographers learned the use of the wet plate; it was a vast advance, since it made a negative that could be reproduced endlessly in prints, but it was still a cumbersome, difficult device. With it, as if they understood their role in history, a number of hardy pioneer cameramen recorded the last and perhaps the most colorful stage in America's westward movement.

The task was intricate. First, you coated a glass plate with a wet solution of collodion and potassium iodide, sensitizing it with silver nitrate in a darkroom. Then the plate—which could not be touched with the fingers—was placed in a dark holder with a removable shield. All this had to go into the camera, whereupon the shield was delicately removed. The plate was exposed by removing a lens cap for one to several seconds, then replacing it. The exposed plate was hurried to the darkroom before the emulsion dried, and developed. Any number of problems—dust, wind, movement—could spoil a picture.

Out in the field, one needed considerable baggage, a wagon for a darkroom, and an array of heavy cameras, tripods, glass plates, bottles of chemicals, printing paper. Even clean, fresh water for developing was often lacking, and had to be brought along. Under such circumstances it is not surprising that the wandering photographers wasted very few plates, and carefully arranged every picture before they took it. This necessity is apparent in much of their work: we see things at quiet moments, after the action is over, the living posed, the dead at rest.

The men who took the pictures in this chapter were an odd assortment of war veterans, refugees from other trades and professions, lovers of adventure. You might be a lifelong photographer, like F. Jay Haynes, who was officially appointed to cover the building of the Northern Pacific Railroad; or you might have drifted into it, like Solomon Butcher, an unsuccessful farmer, or Henry Madison Wantland, who got his cameras in a trade. But you had to have a studio, and find somebody to buy your views and your portraits, the latter usually done up in the form of *cartes de visite*. With success, you might open branch studios, or go along with a government expedition, like J. K. Hillers with John Wesley Powell on his perilous trip down the Colorado River. Best of all, you might acquire your own Pullman photographic car, as Haynes did.

The picture on the opposite page was taken by perhaps the greatest of all the photographers in that wild landscape, William Henry Jackson. Jackson arrived in Omaha, Nebraska, in 1867. He got there as a teamster, but soon had a photographic studio going. On a work train he made his way to Promontory Point to cover the last-spike ceremony. A year later, in 1870, he joined the Hayden Survey Expedition, accompanied by a mule named Hypo, to carry his supplies. He was the first to photograph Yellowstone, and Pikes Peak; a generation knew him by his stereoscopic views of the wild country and raw new towns. He had always been a sketch artist as well, and later in a life that spanned ninety-nine years he took to painting the scenes he had witnessed and photographed, leaving a record of Western reporting that no man has equalled.

Vistas broad enough for any man greet two members of the Hayden Survey party in Wyoming in 1871. They are at Devil's Gate, and in the distance, beyond their wagon, the Sweetwater River plains stretch westward into infinity. This is one of William Henry Jackson's official photographs.

NATIONAL ARCHIVES, GEOLOGICAL SURVEY

OVERLEAF: *These towering red sandstone walls house prehistoric ruins, but this unhappy traveller of 1903 is indifferent to culture as he contemplates his dismembered wagon. The pieces, we are told, were all saved. The scene is the Navajo Indian Reservation in Arizona, in the Canyon de Chelly.*

NATIONAL ARCHIVES

Life in the new Western country was full of danger and death, as these unforgettable photographs testify. At left, their faces full of terror and despair over the deaths of husbands, wives, and children, are fugitives from the great Minnesota Sioux uprising of 1862, which claimed the lives of some 800 settlers and soldiers before Chief Little Crow and his savage followers were defeated, killed, or driven further West. These are survivors from the Riggs and Williamson missions near the Upper Agency, taken while resting during flight by J. E. Whitney, with a stereoscopic camera. Whitney had arrived in the West the day before the massacres began, in hopes of "getting views of Indian life." The picture below, taken by Indian portraitist William S. Soule, has more to say about the grim reality of Western life than a hundred cinematic melodramas. The dead man was Ralph Morrison, a hunter killed and scalped by Indians near Fort Dodge, Kansas, in 1869. His body is shown being discovered by Lieutenant Reade, Third Infantry, and John O. Austin, a frontiersman.

SMITHSONIAN INSTITUTION, BUREAU OF AMERICAN ETHNOLOGY

NATIONAL ARCHIVES, GEOLOGICAL SURVEY

Wayside graves like this one, for soldiers, scouts, and travellers on the Oregon Trail, reminded all who passed of the price the ever-westering Anglo-Saxon had to pay for his new empire on the American frontier. The protective fence around the grave of this soldier, killed near Three Crossings Station in

Colorado in 1862, must have been an affectionate tribute from his friends, in an attempt to fend off coyotes and other scavengers. Here, in a photograph taken some ten years later by William Henry Jackson, the Hayden Survey artist Sanford R. Gifford leans over the fence to study the inscription.

The Frontier West, like all legendary countries, produced heroes — General Custer and Brigham Young, Buffalo Bill and Jesse James. We offer a less remembered but more notable man of action named John Wesley Powell, son of a Methodist exhorter, who became first a botanist, then a soldier (losing his right arm at Shiloh), and finally a truly daring explorer. In 1869 this intrepid man and a small party, financed by the Smithsonian Institution, embarked on the tumultuous Green River and sped down it into the dangerous and little-known Colorado, and at length emerged safely from the Grand Canyon, to the amazement of the Indians, having travelled almost 900 miles. Below we see Powell on the actual expedition, with Tau-gu, a chief of the Paiutes, and at right he appears—as fashion then required—in a stylized studio pose of 1875, against a painted backdrop. From left to right, this preposterous quartet comprises Powell (a major now); Wild Hank Sharp; Kentucky Mountain Bill; and Jesus Alviso, an interpreter who knew Navajo. The studio, the Smithsonian believes, was in Washington.

U. S. GEOLOGICAL SURVEY, PHOTO BY J. K. HILLERS

SMITHSONIAN INSTITUTION

MONTANA HISTORICAL SOCIETY

A mule train arrives in 1874 in Helena, Montana, known ten despairing years earlier as "Last Chance Gulch." Now the town had some 4,000 get-rich-quick inhabitants, and no morals worth mentioning.

Lord, thou hast given me a cell
Wherein to dwell;
A little house, whose humble Roof
Is weather-proof . . .
— ROBERT HERRICK

It was a long, long way from Christiania—or, for that matter, Massachusetts—to the new frontiers of America, nor was the roof always weatherproof. These, the settlers, were the true pioneers, who came for neither gold nor adventure, but to put down their seed and grow with the country. Nebraska was almost treeless, and new arrivals built dugouts like the one at left. You used bundles of willow brush, and hauled timber from the occasional river banks to make windows, doors, and beams, but the main material was sod, cut in long, thick strips. You lived off game and the products of your own toil, you burned buffalo chips, corn cobs, and sunflower stalks, and sometimes, one sod house pioneer lady remembered, a child held an umbrella over you and the skillet while you cooked. You also fought your own war on poverty, unaided, in the wooded states like Wisconsin. In those times, before the unmerciful loggers had almost deforested them, settlers like Nels Wickstrom of Florence County built with logs. Here he is below, posing with his family for an unknown photographer, in 1893. How recent it really is!

STATE HISTORICAL SOCIETY OF WISCONSIN

NEBRASKA STATE HISTORICAL SOCIETY, S. D. BUTCHER COLLECTION

That there were jolly moments on pioneer farms—and that not all sod houses were dugouts—this delightful photograph testifies. It is a stiffly posed watermelon feast, with some disgraceful card-playing thrown in, somewhere in Custer County, Nebraska, taken in the 1880's by S. D. Butcher.

CITY COURT
WHOLESA

BOTH: WESTERN HISTORY COLLECTIONS, UNIVERSITY OF OKLAHOMA LIBRARY

Rush, improvise, get there—these were the watchwords of the new men of the West. Oklahoma had been reserved to the Indians, some of whom were forcibly moved there in the earlier years of the nineteenth century. But the pressure of "boomers" and other would-be settlers finally forced Congress to permit several frenzied land runs. The first began at exactly noon, April 22, 1889, and within a few hours almost two million acres were "settled," or at least claimed, in a mad rush by horse, foot, and buckboard. Oklahoma City, empty prairie at noon, had a population of ten thousand that evening. The scene at the left was immortalized about a month later on a glass plate, probably by Harman T. Swearingen, outside the "city court" of Guthrie. These gentlemen constitute Arbitration Board No. 2, which was to settle many bitter land disputes. Above, a heavily armed party stands by while Houck's Tank, Oklahoma, links up by telegraph with the outside world of 1893. The tank had served cattle drives in the past, but now this area, in the so-called Cherokee Outlet, was also taken over in a land run.

OVERLEAF: *Temporary wooden offices and shops were thrown up shortly after the famous 1889 noontime land run in Oklahoma. H. T. Swearingen photographed these buildings in Guthrie, whose sign painter must have been the busiest man in town!*

WESTERN HISTORY COLLECTIONS, UNIVERSITY OF OKLAHOMA LIBRARY

CITY MARSHALL
OFFICE.
SIGNS
Walker & McCoy
BROKERS
Farm Lands in
AND STATES.
NORTH PARK.
$10 to $20 FINE for cutting any tree or commiting any nuisance in this PARK.
J.M. ENNIS. MAYOR.
J.M. ENNIS MAYOR.

W. M.
ED. S.
DOUGLASS & CLARK
DOUGLASS & CLARK.
LUNCH ROOM AND GROC
ELITE BAKERY.
THURSTON & MERRICK.
ATTY'S and COUNSELORS AT LAW
ROBBINS AND WIER,
REAL ESTATE BROKERS
Bargains in City Lots and Farm Lands in
OKLAHOMA TER. AND STATES
THE
ELITE.
GROCERIES.
PORTERHOUSE STEAK

HAYNES STUDIOS INC.

Not the least of the sights of the frontier was the human show. The new man of the plains, the gulches, and the badlands was a hard-riding, strutting, pistol-packing fellow, a much more colorful production than his drab brethren back East. Some of his womenfolk were rather arresting, too, especially when one recalls that this was the prim height of the Victorian Age. At left we have two tenderfeet, gorgeously gotten up in brand-new Crow Indian suits. F. Jay Haynes, the frontier photographer, has posed them outside of Wild Bill Hickok's house in Deadwood, Dakota Territory. It was 1877, a year after Hickok was murdered there. At right are two citizens of Stillwater, Oklahoma, in the 1890's, posturing as they wished to be remembered for the local photographer, Henry Madison Wantland. The man, a railroad worker, has just drawn his pay and is spruced up for a night on the town. The lady, to stretch that title a little, was one Maggie Montgomery, known locally as "the world's champion cotton picker" and also as a broncobuster and rodeo performer. She was, on the evidence, a snappy dresser, and always carried a riding whip to ward off mashers. Cameraman Wantland himself was an eccentric trader who got into his main career by swapping an old wheat binder for a run-down photographic gallery in Stillwater. He often worked on the barter system, taking goods for his portraits of pioneers and homesteaders.

BOTH: COLLECTION OF ROBERT E. CUNNINGHAM

WESTERN HISTORY DEPARTMENT, DENVER PUBLIC LIBRARY

Give a man a chance and he will set up a refuge for the thirsty before any other structure; the saloon was generally the first edifice to rise in any frontier or mining town. We have one example below, an offense to proper sensibilities that was photographed in the eighties by F. Jay Haynes in Soda Butte Valley, Montana Territory. At left is a fine picture taken during a photographic expedition along the San Miguel River, near Pinon, Colorado, on July 17, 1897. The photographer was an enterprising man named Thomas McKee, who ran galleries variously at Montrose and Ouray, Colorado, and took up the study of painting, paleontology, the Ute Indians, minerals, and, later, the infant field of X ray. Here his group has halted at a place wryly christened "Ocean Grove." The signs are no doubt terribly funny, and we can only admire the straight faces preserved by all.

OVERLEAF: *Here, under a beautiful cloud formation, is plain unadorned Moro, Oregon, population 1,792, about 1890, taken by W. A. Raymond. Lewis and Clark glimpsed this site in 1805, but the first homesteaders only came in 1882—forty of them, attracted by land at $1.25 an acre. They grew Crookneck and Red Chaff wheat and prospered. By 1888 Moro was the county seat, with two churches, a railroad spur, and the knowledge that civilization had come to stay. The frontier (as the professors would soon point out) was finished.*

THE BETTMANN ARCHIVE

HAYNES STUDIOS INC.

GREAT NORTHERN
O.R.& N.

The Displaced Race

The opening of the West and the closing of the frontier, while they cemented the continental power of the United States, brought a tragic end to the long story of the American Indian. Pushed ever westward by the advancing white man and his superior technology, the red man still dominated the plains and mountains at the end of the Civil War. His war bonnet and his scalping knife excited the fears and animated the hostility of the white man until, by the turn of the century, the aboriginal American was removed as an effective force throughout that endless empire which stretched from the Mississippi to the Pacific. By 1900 his numbers were reduced to one third of those who had greeted the first English settlers three centuries before. Canada's Indian policy was a little more humane than ours, and Mexico's was such that the natives at length swallowed up the Spaniards, but here in the United States they became a displaced race.

The Indian wars of the latter half of the last century, now celebrated almost every night on television, were fought, first, to get the Indians on to reservations, and second, to keep them there. The Indians themselves had, of course, no desire to be confined; the white man's ideas of land ownership seemed to them incomprehensible, and actual Indian-agent practice in the West was often a far cry from the usually well-meant policies enunciated in Washington. Robbed and cheated, they rebelled in one last-ditch stand after another. Between 1866 and 1875 more than two hundred battles took place—small ones by modern standards, on the platoon or battalion level—mostly with the Sioux. But the Indians were fragmented, and there were separate battles with the Modocs, the Apaches, the Nez Perces, the Bannocks, the Navajos. The Sioux wiped out Custer and his detachment in 1876, and were themselves put out of action in 1890, when Chief Sitting Bull was murdered and the Ghost Dance movement was suppressed at the Battle of Wounded Knee. (The "battle" was little more than an unprovoked massacre.)

The camera, arriving on this troubled yet thrilling scene about 1865, was (if one may so characterize an inanimate object) of two minds, or perhaps more, on the subject. It showed the red men defeated, or dead—"good Indians," in the phrase of the time. It pictured also those who survived on the white man's terms—degraded, lazy, attired (sometimes ludicrously) in the clothing of their conquerors. Travelling among them, Horace Greeley was unimpressed: *To the prosaic observer, the average Indian of the woods and prairies is a being who does little credit to human nature—a slave of appetite and sloth, never emancipated from the tyranny of one animal passion save by the more ravenous demands of another. As I passed over the magnificent bottoms of the Kansas which form the reservations of the Delawares, Potawatamies, etc., constituting the very best corn-lands on earth, and saw their owners sitting around the doors of their lodges at the height of the planting season and in as good, bright planting weather as sun and soil ever made, I could not help saying, "These people must die out—there is no help for them. . . ."*

Another view, however, is reflected in much of the photography of that era. It was a more thoughtful, modern outlook that saw dignity in the stoic faces of chiefs and braves and strove to make a record of a fast-vanishing culture. The new attitude stirred the famous William Henry Jackson, who is shown at left photographing the Laguna Pueblo in New Mexico. It caught the rapt attention of William Stinson Soule, who was so successful in persuading the proud Indian to pose for "the glass eye in the black box" that his collection of plates is a priceless anthropological record. And it inspired the all-consuming career of Edward S. Curtis, an ambitious practitioner of the new school of "art" photography, who set out at the turn of the century to record in twenty enormous volumes (at $3,000 a set for the first edition) the life of the Indian as it could still be seen. Curtis was backed not only by large donations from J. Pierpont Morgan but by the enthusiastic support of Theodore Roosevelt, who wrote that the Indian as he had been was passing from sight, and that this was the last chance to record him truthfully. He said: *In Mr. Curtis we have both an artist and a trained observer, whose pictures are pictures, not merely photographs; whose work has far more than mere accuracy, because it is truthful.*

Perhaps Mr. Roosevelt was a romantic, but he seems to have perceived a few facts about the new art of photography, its possibilities, and its future.

COLLECTION OF ROBERT A. WEINSTEIN

Something of the mystery and drama of the American Indian comes through in Edward S. Curtis' carefully photographed picture of the Navajos. It was President Theodore Roosevelt's favorite shot.

OVERLEAF: *In another of Curtis' evocative photographs of the vanishing Indian, a small party of Navajos rides through the Canyon de Chelly* (see pp. 62-63). *Its walls in places rise 1,200 feet.*

SEATTLE PUBLIC LIBRARY

WESTERN HISTORY COLLECTIONS, UNIVERSITY OF OKLAHOMA LIBRARY

During one of the last pathetic moments of Indian resistance, Cheyenne and Arapaho tribesmen do the Ghost Dance by the North Canadian River, near Fort Reno, Oklahoma Territory, in August, 1889.

WESTERN HISTORY COLLECTIONS, UNIVERSITY OF OKLAHOMA LIBRARY

The Indian fell back before the stronger medicine of the white man, his technology, his numbers. And the U. S. Army, in the great days of frontier fighting, made use of the old rule of divide and conquer. This picture, taken by the pioneer Oklahoma photographer J. A. Shuck, helps prove that point, for these uniformed Indian scouts are members of the same tribes who are doing the Ghost Dance on the preceding two pages. The Ghost Dancers believed that the Great Spirit would soon make a new world free of white men, that he would fill it again with buffalo and resurrect the Indians who had died, and that those who wore the Ghost Dancer's shirt were safe from bullets. Perhaps these Cheyenne and Arapaho scouts knew better, for they served the Army loyally; Indian scouts were part of the force that next year put an end to the movement in the massacre of 300 Sioux men, women, and children at Wounded Knee Creek, South Dakota, on December 29, 1890.

GLENBOW FOUNDATION

The Indian's natural gravity and dignity made him an ideal subject for portraits. Yellow Rodge, above, of the Sarcee Tribe of the Blackfeet, was photographed about 1887 by W. H. Boone, in Alberta. In 1869 W. S. Soule made the portrait at right of Heap Wolves, a Comanche, handsomely bedecked in a necklace of bone. The hard-riding, hard-fighting Comanches made their home in the Western Plains, until the Texans nearly exterminated them.

OVERLEAF: *Adam Clark Vroman, the amateur photographer who took this picture in about 1904, called it "Two American Indian Madonnas." The women are Southwestern pueblo dwellers, carrying their water jars gracefully balanced on their heads. First a railroad man, later a bookseller, Vroman travelled extensively throughout the Southwest, and often took out his camera to record the lives of the Hopi, the Zuñi, the Pueblos, and other tribes.*

The German word Kulturkampf, *a struggle between cultures, is strangely fitting for these two interesting photographs. Observe below the clash of East and West: two Presbyterian women missionaries, in their severe Sunday black, have come to scrutinize an Apache centenarian at an Indian camp near Anadarko, Oklahoma Territory, in 1898. What message, we wonder, did they bring from Galilee to the old savage? Did she, in return, ask for firewater, or a pinch of snuff? Did the ladies, perhaps, engage her in what today is called a "meaningful dialogue"? All we know for certain is that Mrs. Charles Hume, wife of the doctor to the Kiowa Agency, took the picture. On the right is another strange and melancholy photograph from the American* Kulturkampf, *taken in 1899 by the eminent Frances Benjamin Johnston at Hampton Institute in Virginia. Hampton, founded in 1868 by an idealist named Samuel Chapman Armstrong to help adjust the Negro to freedom, also educated many Indians. Here one of them poses in full regalia, to be studied by his fellow students, most of them Negroes. The typical Indian thought himself better than anyone, white or black: he had never been a slave; and, in fact, he had held white men in that unhappy state. What is in this boy's mind, and in the minds of his beholders?*

WESTERN HISTORY COLLECTIONS, UNIVERSITY OF OKLAHOMA LIBRARY

THE MUSEUM OF MODERN ART, NEW YORK, GIFT OF LINCOLN KIRSTEIN

The Indian leaves two images behind, shown in all-too-bitter contrast in this pair of pictures. At left, in another carefully arranged portrait by Edward S. Curtis, is a Sioux warrior in all his feathers and war paint—but taken in 1905, a good fifteen years after the last battle his tribe ever fought. The Indian's real condition at the turn of the century, unfortunately, is much more accurately reflected by the pathetic old woman below. She is the Princess Angelina, daughter of Chief Seattle, for whom a great city was named. When F. Jay Haynes took this photograph in 1890 Angelina was old and poverty-stricken, living in a hovel in the domain her people had owned and her father had ruled.

HAYNES STUDIOS INC.

SEATTLE PUBLIC LIBRARY

Getting There

Nothing dominates nineteenth-century America like the steam engine, whose effigy should stand in every park, beside the Civil War soldier and the Minuteman, as a prime mover in our history. It found us dependent on the horse and the sail, and it left us only at the beginning of the age of space. It brought a revolution in transportation which knit the enormous continent into one and made us a nation of travellers, even though we have ungratefully forsaken the railway and the steamboat for the automobile and the jet.

The camera was not at hand to witness the birth of steam in England, or the triumphs of Watt, Trevithick, and the Stephensons, father and son. It could not record the transformation in 1806 of Fulton's Folly into Fulton's triumph, or the first hesitant, clanking success of the *Stourbridge Lion,* an English-built locomotive which inaugurated the steam age on American rails with a short successful run at Honesdale, Pennsylvania, in 1829. When the first daguerreotypist ventured out to immortalize the monster on metal a decade or more later it was too late to catch the early stages—the carriages which looked like Concord coaches on flanged wheels, the tiny teakettles like the *De Witt Clinton,* the *Tom Thumb,* and the *Best Friend of Charleston.* Because so much has been lost, because so much was never properly labelled and identified for posterity, it is not possible to lay hands with any certainty on the first photograph of a railroad train, but there are millions of images in every medium that come down to us from those colorful days of steam.

When the railroad crossed a river, from the clear Connecticut to the muddy Mississippi, the camera was there to record it—when it burst into your village there was a parade, led by a hero of the Mexican or Civil War, and a speech by a local Pericles, all preserved on glass. When it steamed up Mount Washington on cogs, its picture (left) was taken—and this train still runs, even if we have lost the Twentieth Century Limited.

By the time of the Civil War, the North had 20,000 miles of track, linked together in a system which served the Union well, but the Southern railroads, with only 9,000, were fragmented—which made a considerable difference, even though the generals at first failed (as they usually do) to comprehend the utility of a new device. The photographers knew better. Brady, Gardner, and O'Sullivan were fascinated by the role of railroads in the conflict, and aimed their lenses at roundhouses, guns mounted on flatcars, and the high, spidery viaducts that General Herman Haupt's military railroadmen threw up, sometimes almost overnight, to get the men and the supplies where they were needed.

After the war was over, photographers like Jackson and Haynes followed the building parties driving westward across the plains and mountains. They loved the deep cuts, the teetering bridges, the dramatic wrecks, the snowsheds, the Gothic depots, the ceremonies. When the last spike was driven at Promontory, Charles R. Savage's pictures were so truthful, so full of bottle-waving workmen and ladies of unknown reputation, that Collis P. Huntington of the Southern Pacific had an accommodating artist make a painting of the scene with the coarser elements eliminated.

No photographer was at hand to capture the first faltering, explosive moments of Ransom E. Olds's merry Oldsmobile, or of Henry Ford's first Lizzie, but there are plenty of photographs of early automobilists to move our own generation to mirth. The high, swaying motorcar of the 1900's soon began to draw the curtain on the long reign of the horse, and it went on to do in the trolley car, the steamboat (at least on rivers and sounds), and finally the lordly train. Our book closes its history just before the First World War, when railroads hauled 85 per cent of the freight and most of the intercity passengers in the country, one billion travellers a year. Now, with one crack passenger train after another sounding its last whistle, railroads are down to less than half the freight and almost no passengers at all, save commuters. The train's place has been usurped by lumbering trucks and by the device of those two bicycle mechanics, Orville and Wilbur Wright: it took off, in its wobbly way, one December day in 1903, and had a portentous future. It is significant that the Wrights were the first to see to it, as we show on page 151, that the moment of triumph was frozen on film, to convince the skeptical and also, perhaps, to preserve it for history.

HENRY E. HUNTINGTON LIBRARY

A thousand forms of ingenuity, most of them devised within the age of photography, made modern transportation possible. For the seasonal, capricious rivers of the West, for example, wire ferries were

often a cheap, practical answer. This one, photographed probably by C. C. Pierce of Los Angeles, crossed the Little Colorado in Arizona. The ladies sit. But what does the covered wagon do?

GEORGE EASTMAN HOUSE COLLECTION

Early railways, especially those before the Civil War, look to us like quaint toys, but the crew of this Boston, Concord & Montreal train were proud enough of their new bridge to pose for a stereograph by the well-known Kilburn brothers of Littleton, New Hampshire. This wooden suspension bridge uses a truss invented by the famous builder Theodore Burr. Trains went over on top, and wagons used the inside. It crossed the Connecticut River from Woodsville, New Hampshire, to Wells River, Vermont, and was completed in 1852, after a near pitched battle between B.C.&M. laborers and the crews of the Passumpsic River Railroad on the other side, which didn't want the bridge built. Railroads were the wave of the future, and canals, most of them constructed only a few decades earlier, were falling into disuse. The Chesapeake and Ohio (below) was already attracting antiquarians when this photograph was taken in 1881 by S. Fisher Corlies.

HAYNES STUDIOS INC.

The West was a challenge to which, as Professor Toynbee might have it, the railroads furnished a great—indeed, romantic—response in the latter half of the nineteenth century, when thin lines of steel threaded their way across the endless prairies and mountains and filled Indian hearts with foreboding. The older picture is the stereograph below, taken by John Carbutt of Chicago during an excursion to the 100th meridian on the Union Pacific Railroad in October, 1866. The race to knit the coasts together by steam had begun—the U. P. building west across the plains, the Central Pacific building east from California, until they met at Promontory, Utah, in 1869. At the time of this picture the rails had reached a point some 250 miles west of Omaha, Nebraska, but the sleepers, which must always be laid first, stretched out beyond them into the setting sun. This picture of an unidentified man standing among them has a strange emotional impact. Just behind him, not visible here, were cars full of Eastern capitalists, newspapermen, European noblemen, U. P. directors, several chefs, and two brass bands. At left, in quite different country, the Northern Pacific crosses a gulch in the early 1880's, on a frightening all-wooden trestle. The photographer was F. Jay Haynes, whose biographer, Freeman Tilden, tells us in Following the Frontier *that this crew posed for Haynes beside an engine and the pay car—the most important bit of consist on the line.*

OVERLEAF: *Railroads could go almost anywhere. This is the Pikes Peak rack railway, photographed by W. H. Jackson rounding Windy Point in its early days. The mountain is 14,110 feet high; the cars are pushed up gradients as steep as one in four along a nine-mile route, much of which has been blasted out of solid rock.*

WESTERN HISTORY DEPARTMENT, DENVER PUBLIC LIBRARY

LIBRARY OF CONGRESS

MANITOU & PIKES PEAK RY.
JOHN HULBERT

The camera caught not only the triumphs but the difficulties and tragedies of railroading. Immediately below is a detail from a stereograph of a disaster on the Wabash at Litchfield, Illinois, on July 3, 1904; a train which had started late from Chicago to St. Louis was making up time when it hit an open switch. The resulting pile-up and fire, which cost nineteen lives, has no great historic consequence—it does not even make the list of "worst accidents" and the railway would never, in any event, match the airplane as a killer—but it typifies the era when larger, heavier equipment was appearing on American railroads that were not ready for it. Nature, too, conspired against the companies. Below, twisted rails and wrecked passenger cars show what a flash flood did to a circus train at Mandan, North Dakota, in 1913. At right we have the problem of snow, against which all Pacific railroads fought. These three engines are deeply buried near the Dalles, east of Portland, Oregon, on the edge of the Cascade Range.

LIBRARY OF CONGRESS

BOTH: STATE HISTORICAL SOCIETY OF WISCONSIN

Portrayed here is a proud but ironic moment in the career of Henry Villard, the German immigrant railroad magnate who pushed the Northern Pacific through to Oregon. The scene is St. Paul, Minnesota, in September, 1883. Villard, who stands forward and hatless on the footboard of a giant American-style 4-4-0 locomotive, was starting a great four-train "last-spike" ceremony and promotional excursion to the West Coast. Forty carloads of financiers and solons would be so impressed, Villard believed, that he could raise some much-needed capital. But it didn't work out that way. The Easterners were bored by the endless flatlands and frightened by the Indians; en route they sold more and more stock at each stop, and Villard for a time lost control of the company. The picture was taken by F. Jay Haynes.

OVERLEAF: *This splendid collection of hats, mustaches, and watch chains, taken by an unknown photographer, belongs to the august clerks of a railroad which, despite its thundering title, never came anywhere near crossing the continent. You used "connections." The Atlantic & Pacific Railroad collapsed in the Panic of 1873 and was later reorganized as the St. Louis & San Francisco Railroad, or Frisco Road, to a large extent a satrapy of Collis P. Huntington, the richest of the Western railway kings. His name graces Good Works today but one contemporary said he had "no more soul than a shark." When whatever soul there was took wing, the fortune turned out to be left to Huntington's nephew Henry, and, since railroads were important affairs in those days, Henry assured his control by marrying his uncle's widow.*

BANCROFT LIBRARY

HAYNES STUDIOS INC.

N.P.R.R.
St. PAUL
MINNESOTA
TO
PORTLAND
OREGON.

ATLANTIC
OVERLAND
AND
OFFICE.
THROUGH RATES
TO
EAST.
4
ATLANTIC
&
PACIFIC R.R.
ATCHISON,
TOPEKA &
SANTA FÉ R.R.
ST. LOUIS &
SAN FRANCISCO
JOHN L. TRUSLOW.
Nº 4
OVERLAND
PASSENGER OFFICE.
"ALL THE YEAR"
ATLANTIC & PACIFIC
TICKETS TO
ALL POINTS EAST.

ET & FREIGHT OFFICE
& PACIFIC R.R.
4
ATLANTIC & PACIFIC
FAST FREIGHT LINE
TO AND FROM
STERN POINTS.
W. A. BISSELL.
Pacific Coast Freight Agt.
QUICK TIME &
THROUGH RATES.

As railroads grew in power and majesty, they attempted on occasion to erect great stations. Here is the old Grand Central Station, which went up between 1869 and 1871 on 42nd Street in New York City, paid for by Commodore Vanderbilt as the grand terminus of his New York Central system. The exterior façade, below, was thought to echo the Louvre; it was designed by architects blessed with the names of Isaac C. Buckhout and John B. Snook. The interior, a truly dramatic train shed, was modelled on—and was almost as large as—St. Pancras Station in London. At the time it covered the largest interior space in America, kept reasonably clean by "flying" (that is, coasting) the passenger cars in, without locomotives. Only at the moment a train was to leave would the smoky engine come into the shed, couple up, and pull out, without using bells or whistles. The second and present Grand Central replaced this wonderful old pile on the same site in the years 1903-1912. The photographer of the outside is anonymous, but the man who took the fine interior was an optician named T. H. McAllister.

BOTH: COLLECTION OF DAVID HOFFMAN

Assembled in great numbers, railway engines and steamboats take on a strange power and excitement. At right, for example, we have a fine scene at the Kansas Pacific Roundhouse No. 8, at Armstrong, Kansas, in 1873. The engines, whose job was chiefly to haul cattle from Abilene to Chicago, have an air of pride in this photograph by Robert Benecke of St. Louis. They amount to something, like the Grenadier Guards or the Marines, and they make it clear that inanimate things can breathe and accomplish great deeds. So, too, do the steamboats seen in the picture above; they also helped open the West in their time. These were assembled at Pittsburgh in 1911, the hundredth anniversary of the first steamboat on the Western rivers, the New Orleans, *built by Nicholas Roosevelt with assistance from Robert Fulton and Robert Livingston. A replica of the old craft lies next to the* Virginia *(whose gangplank is down). Pittsburgh's Mayor W. A. Magee took President Taft to the deck of the* New Orleans *for a speech, and Alice Roosevelt Longworth, a descendant of old Nicholas, christened the replica. R. W. Johnston climbed a telephone pole to take this picture saluting a means of passenger transportation that would soon disappear almost entirely from the face of the land. Carrying goods, both riverboats and railroads would, apparently, keep on rolling along.*

CARNEGIE LIBRARY OF PITTSBURGH

COLLECTION OF FRED AND JO MAZZULLA

LIBRARY OF CONGRESS

At the left is a typical Mississippi passenger and freight packet backing off a bank with a load of cotton, her landing stage planks pulled up. Like most boats on the shallow Western rivers, she is a stern-wheeler. Built in 1884, the Pargoud *ended her career about 1898, and was photographed in between by A. D. Lytle. Hear Mark Twain on those days, from* Life on the Mississippi: *"... the great Mississippi, the majestic, the magnificent Mississippi, rolling its mile-wide tide along, shining in the sun ... the 'point' above the town, and the 'point' below, bounding the river-glimpse ... Presently a film of dark smoke appears above one of those remote 'points'; instantly a Negro drayman, famous for his quick eye and prodigious voice, lifts up the cry, 'S-t-e-a-m-boat a-comin'!' and the scene changes! The town drunkard stirs, the clerks wake up, a furious clatter of drays follows, every house and store pours out a human contribution, and all in a twinkling the dead town is alive and moving. Drays, carts, men, boys, all go hurrying from many quarters to a common center, the wharf...." Below, jam-packed with people rather than cargo, is an Eastern side-wheeler, the* John Sylvester, *whose fine vertical (or "walking") beam engine and solid hull kept her running from 1866 to 1931, in places as far-flung as Florida, the James River, and Long Island Sound.*

OVERLEAF: *Still another kind of steamboating comes to life again in this photograph of a stern-wheeler of the Hart Line, probably the* Okeehumkee, *arriving one day in 1886 at Silver Springs, Florida, after an overnight run up the St. Johns, Oklawaha, and Silver rivers. The paddle wheels of the Oklawaha steamers were so deeply recessed as to be almost invisible, so that at first glance the craft appeared to be screw propelled. The service ran from 1860 to 1920, and was a great tourist attraction.*

LIBRARY OF CONGRESS

SMITHSONIAN INSTITUTION

Nothing brings back America's great seafaring days more sharply than early photographs of the waterfront. At left is a view of the docks at New Bedford, taken about 1880. The whaling bark Massachusetts *is drying her sails, and behind her is moored a "ship," that is, a vessel whose three masts are all square-rigged. On the wharf you could still see and smell the casks of whale oil, but the days of whaling were drawing to a close by the 1880's. Too many of the ships had been sunk by Confederate raiders, or by the Federal government in its wartime attempt to block the port of Charleston, South Carolina. Then, too, oil was being taken from the ground in ever-increasing quantities. Below is a stereograph taken on July 30, 1873, by J. Freeman, who wrote one puzzling word on the back: "Minmaneth." Is this the vessel's name? Why has she got her sails set so dangerously close to shore? Is she beached? Are those sacks cargo, taken ashore to lighten the ship? Are the respectable onlookers picnickers, kibitzers, or perhaps a prospective salvage party? Sometimes old photographs have a way of raising more questions than they answer.*

OVERLEAF: *This picture by Alice Austen, the noted Staten Island photographer, shows ships loading and unloading cargo at a dock on South Street, New York City. At right, astern of the German merchantman* J. W. Gildemeister, *is the full-rigged ship* Canada. *Visible behind the German's mast is a Brooklyn-Manhattan ferry; a jaunty type in a bowler hat adds an ineffable touch.*

STATEN ISLAND HISTORICAL SOCIETY

GEORGE EASTMAN HOUSE COLLECTION

SAMSON

Their rigging delicately webbed with snow, lumber barks (left) and schooners (right) lie at the loading docks of Port Blakely, on Puget Sound, Washington, in the winter of 1905. This is one of a great collection of glass plates made by Wilhelm Hester, a frontier marine photographer born in Germany.

SAN FRANCISCO MARITIME MUSEUM, HESTER COLLECTION

OVERLEAF: *Under bare poles, a bark out of Nantes, France, comes across the bar at the mouth of the Columbia River. Captain Orison Beaton of the tug* Goliah, *which was towing the Frenchman, took this spectacular picture through a port just before the huge wave crashed over his vessel.*

SAN FRANCISCO MARITIME MUSEUM, PLUMMER COLLECTION

CAPE COD PHOTOS

The weather was clear when the fishing schooner Fortuna *sailed from Gloucester, Massachusetts, on Lincoln's Birthday, 1894, but she ran out of fortune and into foul weather and went aground on Cape Cod's treacherous shoals. The wreck conveniently occurred in front of the Race Point Station of the*

U.S. Life Saving Service, and help came within minutes—but two men died, and the Fortuna's *career was finished six months after it began. Irving L. Rosenthal, a Provincetown portrait photographer who liked to take reportorial pictures as well, showed the wreckage being stripped by scavengers.*

NATIONAL ARCHIVES

These two panoramic photographs, taken in the great empty vistas of the West, somehow symbolize the twentieth-century transportation revolution on the roads—or what were regarded as roads in 1900. (There were only some two hundred miles of hard-surfaced pike outside of cities in the whole country in that year.) The box buggy above was taken on the Chisum Ranch of J. J. Hagerman, near Roswell, New Mexico, in 1903; but the long

reign of the horse was then swiftly drawing to a close. The dusty touring car below was photographed about ten years later, while stopped by a much-amended sign showing the way to Laramie, Wyoming. The picture was taken by Sidney D. Waldron, an enterprising early official of the American Automobile Association who made several pathfinding trips across the continent before the comfortable days of asphalt and route numbers.

AMERICAN AUTOMOBILE ASSOCIATION

PENNELL COLLECTION, UNIVERSITY OF KANSAS

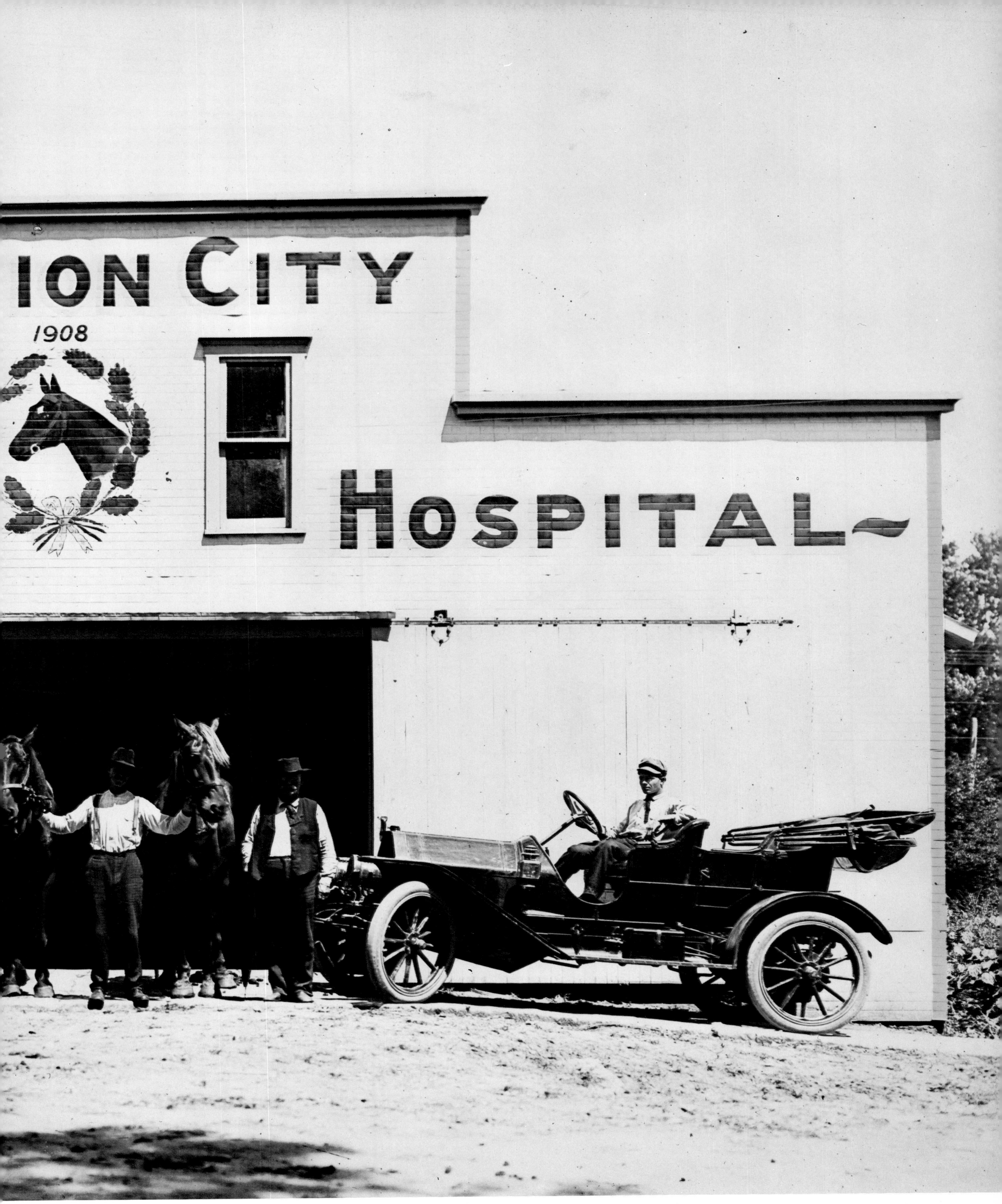

Life was changing at the veterinary hospital in Junction City, Kansas, when Joseph J. Pennell took this picture in 1909. The white-suited gentleman must be the vet, Doctor Hopkins. With somewhat pointed symbolism Pennell has added a lady in a four-wheeler and the proud driver of a new motor car.

AMERICAN AUTOMOBILE ASSOCIATION

Difficulties, accidents, the unexpected were the lot of the early automobilists. At left, a 1903 Packard has developed a puncture, possibly from driving along the railroad track. Below, a car stuck in deep mud draws stares but not much help from the drivers of passing buggies. The picture is from an album of a cross-country trip made around 1902 by one Tom Fetch, but the locale is not indicated. At right is a somber group photographed around a ditched Model T Ford by W. D. Orr, in 1914. "A sudden plunge, yet an undamaged Ford," reads his cheerful caption. Could this be a staged picture?

AMERICAN AUTOMOBILE ASSOCIATION

LIBRARY OF CONGRESS

LIBRARY OF CONGRESS

The early days of transportation are spiced with comic photographs, although not all of them were planned that way. The aeroplane had not been long on the scene before the fearless aeronaut summoned the photographer, settled his wife (or other female relative) at the al fresco *controls, and had her picture taken, regardless of her costume. We cannot identify the lady at left or, for that matter, the natty motorist below drawing water from a rather mysterious pipe. Is there a pump behind the tree? His rig is a brand-new Locomobile steam-car of about 1905, with a tiller to steer by, bicycle wheels, and a water tank in back. And he has a pair of rubbers on the floor, ready for any emergency.*

LIBRARY OF CONGRESS, WILLIAM MILLER COLLECTION

CHICAGO HISTORICAL SOCIETY

The idea that man could fly, under power, in something heavier than air was a popular one in the 1890's and early 1900's, but not every device got off the ground. This one, a sixteen-disc

"helicopter," is one of various nonflying machines built by James F. Scott, a Chicago artist. It fluttered and trembled and stayed, to its creator's helpless consternation, exactly where it was.

LIBRARY OF CONGRESS

The International Ballooning Contest at Aero Park, Chicago, gets ready for the start on July 4, 1908; the wind blew the winner 895 miles to West Shefford, Quebec, almost a day later. Balloon races were immensely popular and drew vast crowds.

The photographer, George Raymond Lawrence, was passionately dedicated to taking photographs from balloons, and doubtless this is an early example of his aerial exploits. He also built the giant camera which is pictured on the title page.

BOTH: LIBRARY OF CONGRESS

With the wind stinging his face, Wilbur Wright flies in a glider (left) across the deserted beach at Kitty Hawk, North Carolina, on October 10, 1902. He and his brother Orville were sensible, methodical, practical—and inspired. The glider tests went on for several years until, in late 1903, the brothers were ready for the first successful powered flight in a heavier-than-air machine. That exact moment, on December 17, 1903, appears below: the plane has just cleared the launching track into a stiff breeze, with Orville sprawled at the controls. Wilbur, who has run alongside to steady the wing, stops in his tracks to watch in jubilation and, perhaps, awe. The brothers could glimpse a little of what was at stake, and Orville had carefully aimed a camera at the end of the starting rail so that a photograph could be taken by his friend John T. Daniels of the Kill Devil Life Saving Station. When the great day was over, Orville sent the following matter-of-fact telegram to their father in Dayton, Ohio, where the brothers had run a bicycle shop:

SUCCESS FOUR FLIGHTS THURSDAY MORNING ALL AGAINST TWENTY ONE MILE WIND STARTED FROM LEVEL WITH ENGINE POWER ALONE AVERAGE SPEED THROUGH AIR THIRTY ONE MILES LONGEST 57 SECONDS INFORM PRESS HOME FOR CHRISTMAS

Rural America

In the age of megalopolis, when fully 70 per cent of our people live in cities, when the land is laced with superhighways and the air crisscrossed by jets, it is difficult to realize that only a century ago we were an intensely rural people. Three out of four Americans lived in places with fewer than 2,500 inhabitants; well over 50 per cent of the population was engaged in farming, as opposed to less than 6 per cent today. In the fifty years or more recorded here, all this was changing rapidly. Farm acreage was increasing in the absolute sense, to feed a fast-growing population and much of the outside world, but the share of the farmer in the political and social life of the United States was in decline. The country was turning industrial, and behind protective tariff walls everything the farmer bought cost more, while his crops brought in less. Cotton dropped from thirty-one cents a pound in 1866 to six cents in 1893; in almost the same period wheat dropped from a dollar forty-five a bushel to forty-nine cents. Mortgages bought cheap were repaid dear, if they could be paid off at all.

The man who sowed with so much labor and reaped with so little result led the hard, despairing, debt-ridden life that we read about in the works of Hamlin Garland, Ellen Glasgow, and Willa Cather, and glimpse in the pictures that follow. Out of all this hard work, suffering, and cultural deprivation spring a thousand currents of modern times: here are the ancestors of the Populists, the Okies, and the citizens of Sinclair Lewis' Gopher Prairie; here are the intensely moral and narrow people who gave us Prohibition and convicted Scopes in the famous "Monkey" trial in Tennessee, and who later, in California, swarmed into the gilded temple of Aimee Semple McPherson. Look at the background in the barren farm on the next pages; consider W. A. Raymond's pictures of life around Moro, Oregon, Charles Van Schaick's of small Wisconsin towns, or J. J. Pennell's of Kansas. This is where we come from—many of us, at least, whether today we are computer programmers, real estate salesmen, or airline hostesses—and the photographers who covered it were social historians.

The torrent of change has also left behind the more pleasing picture of the village or small town, a world that sometimes seems light years away. The sounds are different, from the beat of horses' hooves to the distant whistle of the morning accommodation train, and so are the scent in the air and the very pace of life. The scene is bathed deep in nostalgia, for this is the national folk memory of a time when things were slower, surer, and ever so much simpler. The flood of immigration was just beginning, and most of it was going to the cities. The gentry were highly regarded and in most places the most important men were the parsons. Before city life fragmented the family the generations lived together, and enjoyed a kind of companionship now largely lost in an age that sets the old aside, out of everyone's way, under the noisome euphemism of "senior citizens."

This irretrievable world lingers on in the work of a number of great photographers, very few of whom probably ever paused to consider that what they were recording would vanish as absolutely as Nineveh and Tyre. Most of the professional photographers were concerned mainly with portraiture, the source of their income: the outdoor scenes, historic moments, and conversation pieces are incidental. Every town had at least one such operative, and, after the invention of the dry plate and the Kodak, a great many amateurs. One of them is at work at left, in about 1882; she is Martha H. Whitney, busily photographing her foster mother and her children.

Nearly all the treasures stored up by amateurs and professionals alike have been broken up, or lost, or used in making greenhouse roofs, leaving us with relatively few notable collections. Among those used in this book are the collections of Arthur J. Telfer who, in a lifetime of ninety-five years, left us a panorama of small-town people and events in rural Cooperstown, New York; Charles Currier, who photographed the life of Boston and its suburbs in exquisite detail, but left very few identifying captions; Chansonetta Stanley Emmons, who did the same for her native village of Kingfield, Maine, but also left little information on her subjects; and a gifted amateur, Leonard Dakin of Cherry Valley, New York, who made an unforgettable record of one well-bred, comfortable family (his own) and then stored away his glass plates, carefully labelled, in a barn, to be resurrected—as the life of the time never can be—some sixty years later.

NATIONAL ARCHIVES

The date and location of this photograph are lost, but it is nonetheless eloquent about prairie farmlife.

NATIONAL ARCHIVES

There is something Biblical, even today, about the tribulations and rewards of the farmer. Behold at left the dismal state of a farm at Leesburg, Virginia, after a bad hailstorm in 1912; the corn is ruined, and the owner might be Job, standing there with folded arms of patient sorrow. He was taken by an anonymous government photographer. His gloom contrasts strikingly with the joy of the old Maine dairyman below, whose kine and fowl are producing well in a land scarcely known for milk and honey. His broad smile was immortalized sometime around the turn of the century by the remarkable New England photographer Chansonetta Stanley Emmons, who specialized in recording the ordinary life of her kith and kin and neighbors in rural Maine.

CULVER PICTURES

The farm and the plantation were still home to the majority of American Negroes after the Civil War as before, and until two world wars brought them to the cities of the North. The classic scene of cotton-picking below, taken by an unknown photographer at Jackson, Tennessee, gives us an idea of what that life was like, and the girl at right, smiling amidst the peanut crop in an anonymous photograph, recalls the classic stereotype of the carefree Negro.

CULVER PICTURES

COOK COLLECTION, THE VALENTINE MUSEUM

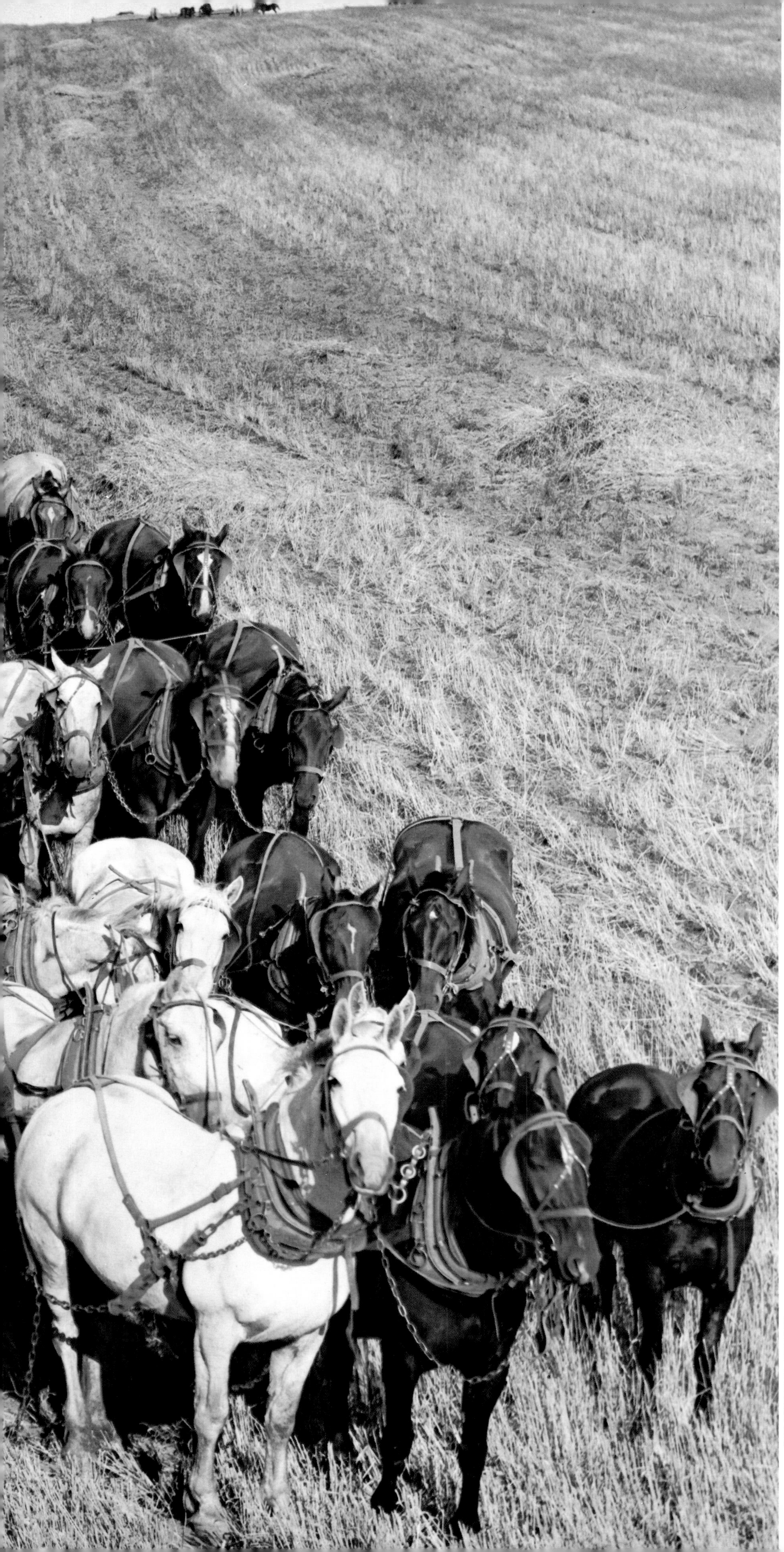

THE BETTMANN ARCHIVE

On the big farms of the Great Plains and the far Northwest mechanical, horse-drawn monsters converted the wide, open spaces into "America's breadbasket." The marvelous combine had been a farmer's dream for generations. Now American inventive talent had made it a reality, joining the work of binding and threshing into one operation and requiring the labor of only three men instead of up to thirty. Pulled slowly through seas of ripened grain by gangs of as many as forty horses, their driver reining the wheel teams from his thronelike perch atop an inclined ladder, the huge machines were also a source of wondrous pictorial drama. Post cards recording this new spectacle of life in the American West were made from photographs like the one at left, taken by W. A. Raymond on an eastern Oregon wheat farm in the late 1880's. Soon afterward, steam began to replace the animals, and by 1912, when gasoline-powered combines appeared, the drama provided by the majestic troops of horses was gone.

STATE HISTORICAL SOCIETY OF WISCONSIN

A rewarding crop of oats as high as a man's eye was something to feel proud about, and one of the favorite ways to record it for posterity was to have it photographed with men who looked as if they were drowning in it. This happy bonanza scene on Edward Dascam's farm at Antigo, Wisconsin,

was made in 1895, probably by J. J. Kingsbury, a local photographer. One can almost hear him directing Farmer Dascam's obliging friends to hold their hats high over their heads so they will not fail to be noticed amid the tall stand of oats, all of it probably raised to fatten up his dairy cows.

CULVER PICTURES

STATEN ISLAND HISTORICAL SOCIETY

Rural New England showed much less change in the new century. The photograph above of the interior of a gristmill in New Portland, Maine, was made by Chansonetta Emmons in the teens, but it could have been taken fifty years earlier. Granite-faced farmers still brought their wheat and corn to the mill to be ground for their own use into flour and "Injun meal," and often paid the miller with a portion of produce rather than with cash. The Alice Austen photograph of 1890 at the right shows an almost timeless scene at the covered Henry Bridge in Bennington, Vermont. Built in the 1830's (and still standing today, although in markedly different surroundings), the bridge's façade served as a billboard for advertising patent medicines and local livestock sales.

OVERLEAF: *A barn-raising was both a good neighborly "one-for-all and all-for-one" undertaking that quickened the growth of parts of agricultural America, and also (when the work was done) an occasion for a social gathering by the families of all the men who had pitched in to help. In this photograph by Theodore Teeple of a barn-raising in 1888 at the farm of Jacob Roher near Massillon, Ohio, the bents, or sections, are up, and the co-operative work is over. The expressions of the men on the newly raised framework (and of the women and children) indicate that the hour of reward—a huge dinner and possibly dancing and singing—is near.*

THE MASSILLON MUSEUM

GREAT AUCTION SALE!
HORSES!
BENNINGTON VT

Memories of the farm were kept ever green by family photographs, and sitting for a group picture was sure to be part of the program of any large gathering of relatives. This family portrait was made

STATE HISTORICAL SOCIETY OF WISCONSIN

about 1890 by Gerhard Gesell, a professional photographer in Alma, Wisconsin, during a visit by some of his wife's relatives. Gesell's oldest son Arnold became the well-known child psychologist.

Devotion had many faces, but not all of them were immediately apparent to the camera. The picture below, for instance, bears on its reverse only the charming notation, "The horse's name is Dick." The man is Dr. Edward A. Bass, for some thirty years after 1870 a rural physician in Monticello, Wisconsin. Presumably those grouped with him on Dick's supply of hay are his family. The doctor was an amateur photographer and may have taken the picture himself by time exposure. The doughty farm couple opposite, Alexander Arries and his wife, were photographed at Burlington, New York, in 1881 by Arthur Telfer, then seventeen, who made the plate by coating a piece of window glass with white of egg.

STATE HISTORICAL SOCIETY OF WISCONSIN

NEW YORK STATE HISTORICAL ASSOCIATION

ALL: CULVER PICTURES

These engaging pictures of farm children playing around a back-yard pump and in the dirt behind a Maine farmhouse were taken by Chansonetta Emmons, who spent a number of summers with a farm family near Kingfield during the early years of this century. She usually tried to catch the uninhibited look of life as it really was, with the kind of happy result seen opposite and above. Occasionally, however, she seemed to succumb to the convention of the day that only the pretty was "artistic"; then the photograph, like the one overleaf of two neatly dressed little girls politely watching an immaculate boy fishing from a skiff at Chesham, New Hampshire, appears posed and unreal, although it beguiles us as a set piece in rural America of yesteryear, idealized, as we would like to remember it.

Reverie and memory were two treasures of the happy, golden years. The meditative gentleman on the opposite page is Charles R. Savage, famed Mormon photographer of Salt Lake City, who for half a century beginning in 1859 took many of the most celebrated pictures of the pioneer American West, including views at Promontory, Utah, on May 10, 1869, of the completion of the first transcontinental railroad. Now it is Christmas Day many years later, and Savage, apparently by time exposure, has recorded the table laid, the Christmas bells and garlands hung, the tree and centerpiece in place, and all, even the baby's high chair, ready in his Salt Lake City home for the arrival of the rest of the family circle. The delightful study of the elderly ladies below, busily chatting over their tatting in the parlor, was taken by Belle Johnson, a professional photographer in Monroe, Missouri.

THE MASSILLON MUSEUM

From the farms all roads led to marketing centers, which were usually the county seats or other small towns. The unpaved country roads, which followed the boundaries of the farms or the contours of the terrain, often twisted like corkscrews and were generally far muddier, dustier, icier, or more pocked with holes and ruts than is even hinted at in the view opposite of a hard-packed road known as the Range Way at New Portland, Maine. The tranquil scene of the horse and buggy, temporarily halted while the driver busies himself on the roadside—perhaps to gather a nosegay for his companion?—was made by Chansonetta Emmons. In winter the roads were not plowed. The snow was simply packed down and sleighs were taken from the stable, or wheels were replaced with runners—and traffic continued, as in the stereographic scene below, made by a Boston photographer known only as D. Barnum, probably in the 1860's. The sleighs were colorful, but they were also quiet and required bells to warn pedestrians of their approach.

GEORGE EASTMAN HOUSE COLLECTION

CULVER PICTURES

In 1847, when the Village of Summerville, South Carolina, was incorporated, one of the founding fathers' chief objectives was to protect its lovely stands of pine trees, and to this day you may not cut down a tree in Summerville without a license. Behind the beautiful pines, water oaks, and live

oaks, draped with Spanish moss, stands a row of graceful old Southern houses on Sumter Avenue, which looks very much the same today. This peaceful scene was taken in 1906, when the town was in its heyday as a popular winter resort—it is still one of the South's most charming villages.

LIBRARY OF CONGRESS, DETROIT PUBLISHING COMPANY COLLECTION

CAFE
INDEPE

BOOTS · RUMMEL
SHOES
RUMMEL & BRICK
INDEPENDENCE MO

INDEPENDENCE KANS

ALL: LIBRARY OF CONGRESS, BANDHOLTZ COLLECTION

At least seven American towns bore the proud name of Independence. Three of them, in Iowa (top), Missouri (center), and Kansas (bottom), were pictured by a Des Moines photographer named Fred J. Bandholtz, who between 1907 and 1910 set up his panoramic camera in the main intersections of a number of small Midwestern towns. These three Independences looked pretty much alike. Trolleys ran along the principal streets of each, but horses still outnumbered the automobiles (only one can be seen in the top picture, a few are parked on the middle street of the center picture, and none are in sight in the bottom view). In the Iowa town, where a sign at far left advertises "the best $3 Hat in the World," there are riders as well as an apparition (second frame from left), which is not a sulky but a horse and wagon that moved too quickly for the camera's exposure. Missouri's Independence was already famous for having been the jumping-off point of the Santa Fe, Oregon, and California Trails. Later, it would acquire added celebrity as the home town of Harry S. Truman, the thirty-third President of the United States, who was twenty-five when this picture was taken in 1909. The Independence of Kansas, the smallest of the three towns, was the home at one time of Alfred M. Landon, who became Governor but missed the Presidency by a landslide.

Many small towns were no more than a single street lined with buildings that provided nearby country people with all their necessities, including the chance to do a little visiting. The popular gathering place, of course, was the post office, a good source of free news and free ink. The one at right is at Lake Clear Junction, New York, photographed by H. M. Beach. The town philosophers reasoned together at the general store, in an atmosphere of fine old aromas. In summer the men sat outside and talked; in the winter they huddled around a potbellied stove inside. The country store in Pentwater, Michigan (left), photographed about 1900 by Carrie Ellen Mears, was typical; its wares included almost everything a farm family might require, from horseshoes and buggy tires to hurricane lamps. The picture below of rustic shoppers in a small Wisconsin town near La Crosse was taken in the 1890's by Charles Van Schaick.

THE ADIRONDACK MUSEUM

STATE HISTORICAL SOCIETY OF WISCONSIN

STATE HISTORICAL SOCIETY OF WISCONSI

Broadway was a tame street, as the song alleged, compared to the main streets of ten thousand small towns—that is, of your own. Main Street was a magnet that attracted anything worth seeing. The flowered hats and latest fashions at left (possibly right straight from Chicago via the mail order catalogue) were definitely worth seeing, and photographer Charles Van Schaick probably had to do no urging to get the ladies on the wooden sidewalk to look at the camera and smile. The time was about 1900, the town is thought to be Black River Falls, Wisconsin, and the flags suggest that it may have been the Fourth of July. At about the same time, another photographer, Henry Wantland, was picturing the lustier main street of Stillwater, Oklahoma (right), a comparatively new frontier town in what was still a U.S. territory. The object to be seen here was, of all things, a newfangled, hand-cranked washing machine. The indefatigable "drummer," in apron and derby hat, has done a load and hung it up, and while it is a good bet that he won't make a sale in this crowd, he has at least provided a show worth photographing. The studio on the right, below, was Wantland's headquarters at Stillwater, when in the 1890's he built up a lively business photographing the local scene and selling prints to homesteaders for cash or for barter.

BOTH: COLLECTION OF ROBERT E. CUNNINGHAM

It was in pictures like those here and on the next two pages that small-town America wished to be remembered. The portrait below of a sober little girl dressed up in hat and laces was taken about 1885 by Arthur Telfer of Cooperstown, New York. The little boy at right, photographed in 1898 by Joseph Pennell, is young Lester Bermant, the son of the proprietor of the Exquisite Bottling Works of Junction City, Kansas, gotten up to look like the heir to an earldom. Poor Lester is a victim of the Fauntleroy craze, when countless boys were costumed in satins and laces to resemble the hero of Mrs. Frances Hodgson Burnett's syrupy romance, Little Lord Fauntleroy. *Little Cedric was sickeningly good, called his mother "Dearest," and did indeed inherit an earldom—remaining all the while thoroughly humble and democratic. The American dream, it seems, is always capacious enough to accommodate a prince or two, a lost dauphin here and there, and a latent nostalgia for the world of titles and nobility.*

NEW YORK STATE HISTORICAL ASSOCIATION

PENNELL COLLECTION, UNIVERSITY OF KANSAS

This snappy gentleman of fashion is named W. L. Taylor, and is thought to have been the town barber of Cooperstown, New York. His portrait was made there by Arthur Telfer around 1885.

The handsome, smartly dressed lady above, another of Telfer's subjects, was probably the wife of W. L. Taylor. Not all American Negroes were downtrodden beings toiling away in the cotton fields.

THE MASSILLON MUSEUM

THE BETTMANN ARCHIVE

The superbly gotten-up dude above was immortalized by Oregon photographer W. A. Raymond in the early 1900's. By the nineties the beard was going out of fashion, but men were still wearing mustaches; you could get all sorts of preparations in plain wrappers that would grow hair on the smoothest face. The ladies were also proud of their crowning glory—a regal thing, no doubt, at all times, but in the picture at left, it has grown to imperial length. These three damsels were photographed by Belle Johnson of Monroe, Missouri. Perhaps they were trying to copy the famous Seven Sutherland Sisters of Niagara County, New York, whose combined hair length was advertised to be thirty-six feet, ten inches; the longest in the world, the sisters claimed.

Religion, or at least that outward form of it often called "that old-time religion," was a strong force in nineteenth-century America, and nowhere did it have a greater effect on people's morals and opinions than in the small towns. As the cities grew bigger, and the urban masses, competing for material gain, appeared to weaken in the unending struggle with the Devil, the rural areas by contrast shone ever brighter as the redoubts of the pieties and virtues with which the country had been built. "Our nation," proclaimed one tormented antisaloon leaguer early in the 1900's, "can only be saved by turning the pure stream of country sentiment and township morals to flush out the cesspools of cities." There was some exaggeration in the image, for small-town America was also a land of Huck Finns of all ages, and most towns of any size (save in states and territories that had voted dry) boasted at least one establishment like the Wisconsin ordinary below, photographed by Charles Van Schaick. But it was also true that the country churches, like armories, were mobilization centers for shock troops of such organizations as the Woman's Christian Temperance Union, whose members, linking strong drink to Satan, would sally forth and, like the "Whirlwind of the Lord," as the saying went, would burst into saloons, where to the horror of the bartender and his clientele they would kneel on the sawdust-covered floor and pray for the destruction of the premises. A sample of what the saloonkeeper was up against may be seen at the right, a flight of W.C.T.U. stormbirds photographed by W. A. Raymond at Moro, about 1900. The presence of the man is unexplained.

OVERLEAF: *Public baptism was a visible sign of the steadfast faith of country people, both black and white, in fundamentalist, pentecostal, and* al fresco *religion. This Negro baptism near Richmond, Virginia, photographed by Heustis Cook about 1896, was typical of the period. The white spectators in that placid, friendly, unequal South of long ago were welcomed as guests.*

COOK COLLECTION, THE VALENTINE MUSEUM

STATE HISTORICAL SOCIETY OF WISCONSIN

THE BETTMANN ARCHIVE

COLLECTION OF DR. ROBERT G. REED

This harsh and Gothic scene, photographed about a century ago near Muncie, Indiana, reminds us how different were the customs of death in the old America. Here are none of the euphemisms and evasions so exquisitely satirized by Evelyn Waugh in The Loved One. *The coffin lid has been removed (outdoors, to get enough light for the unknown photographer) and what may well be the only picture ever made of the departed is being taken. You can almost hear the preacher:* "I am the resurrection and the life, saith the Lord: he that believeth in me . . . ." *It seems safe to suppose that all this stark and grieving company did indeed believe.*

OVERLEAF: *A lonely family burial plot on the Kansas prairie, with Father already at rest in the soil of his adopted country far from his Irish starting point, and a place waiting for Mother, was photographed by J. J. Pennell in 1898. How incredibly bleak it is!*

PENNELL COLLECTION, UNIVERSITY OF KANSAS

IHS
IN MEMORY OF
PATRICK FLANAGAN
BORN
COUNTY ROSCOMMON.
IRELAND
DEC. 25, 1817
DIED
DEC. 31, 1892
REQUIESCAT IN PACE.
FLANAGAN
FATHER

This picture has no title and no explanation. It might be called "The Outing," but where are the people going, or where they have been? Perhaps the little group is simply out for a Sunday stroll along a country lane on a warm day in early spring (or do the trees have the look of Indian

summer late in the autumn?). The unidentified glass plate, made by an unknown photographer, was found at the New Haven Colony Historical Society, and the scene is probably rural Connecticut. From the subjects' clothing it would also appear that the time was about the turn of the century.

NEW HAVEN COLONY HISTORICAL SOCIETY

SOCIETY FOR THE PRESERVATION OF NEW ENGLAND ANTIQUITIES

LIBRARY OF CONGRESS, CURRIER COLLECTION

LIBRARY OF CONGRESS, CURRIER COLLECTION

Many a photographer liked to capture his subjects on the front porch—where the light was much better—and sometimes he was fortunate enough to find an important personage in the group, as in James W. Black's picture, above, of the Haven family of Beverly Farms, Massachusetts. Salmon P. Chase, Lincoln's Secretary of the Treasury, and Chief Justice of the United States when this photograph was made about 1868, is at far right with his host, the Boston financier Franklin Haven. We have no names to go with the eager faces in Charles Currier's picture at the extreme left. Immediately to the left is the same cameraman's photograph of his summer cottage at Little Deer Isle, Maine; his son is at right, front, his wife is in the center. The lad on the roof "makes" the picture.

STATE HISTORICAL SOCIETY OF WISCONSIN

Drowsy summer days with sharply delineated light and shadow were made to order for the nineteenth-century photographer, who frequently pressed his family into service as he tried for special effects. Harry Dankoler, secretary of a mining company and editor of a boys' magazine in Sturgeon Bay, Wisconsin, had an acquiescent wife and a ready hammock (above), but his son Syl seems to have had his mind on something more active than posing for his father. The softly lit scene at right was composed by Leonard Dakin in 1890, at the family summer residence, "Uplawn," in Cherry Valley, New York. Leonard's father, George Dakin, is at left; his wife Jessie holds the baby, Roland; and his brother Paul leans on the rail at the right of the picture.

COLLECTION OF PAULINE DAKIN TAFT

STATEN ISLAND HISTORICAL SOCIETY

STATE HISTORICAL SOCIETY OF WISCONSIN

Scattered throughout rural America were the great houses of the gentry—the old families and the new ones who were eager to join their circle. The elegant structure at left, barely visible behind the smothering ivy and ailanthus, was the twenty-two-room New Brunswick, New Jersey, seat of the Strongs, a family that was descended from three Colonial governors and the New York Van Rensselaers. The house was built in 1870 by Judge Woodbridge Strong, whose demure daughter Bessie may be seen in the background, posed on the porch railing for her friend Alice Austen. No establishment of this size operated effortlessly, of course; belowstairs there was usually a formidable force of hired girls, as shown in the unrelated photograph above, by Charles Van Schaick—the laundresses, cooks, parlor maids, and lowly scullery operatives who made up the household staff of one single establishment.

OVERLEAF: *In a picture of what might be anyone's grandmother's house, nothing was left to chance by the photographer, Charles Currier. The family, the lad with his penny-farthing bicycle, even the house with its shutters so carefully arranged—all seem conscious of the moment.*

LIBRARY OF CONGRESS, CURRIER COLLECTION

COLLECTION OF MARGERY HOFFMAN SMITH

STATE HISTORICAL SOCIETY OF WISCONSIN

In Victorian parlors life was just as staid as the mannered façades suggested. You could, like Mrs. James G. Robbins (left) of Portland, Oregon, tend to your knitting. (The photographer was her niece, Julia E. Hoffman.) Or you could fall asleep over the evening paper, as in the scene of stultifying quiet above, recorded in Wisconsin by Charles Van Schaick. A musical evening—one is pictured below by W. A. Raymond in Moro—was slightly more gay, but not sufficiently so to keep rural youth from fleeing to the city's lights.

THE BETTMANN ARCHIVE

COLLECTION OF ROBERT E. CUNNINGHAM

STATE HISTORICAL SOCIETY OF WISCONSIN

STATE HISTORICAL SOCIETY OF WISCONSIN

Music had charms, and no proper home was without the sound of endlessly rehearsed scales. The reluctant virtuoso opposite, hair neatly parted, dressed in an outfit only a mother could have selected, seems as uncertain as we are as to what note he will extract from an unwilling instrument. Visible behind his chair is the base of a headrest, used by this photographer, Henry Wantland, long after most of his colleagues had abandoned them. What strains filled the air in the outing at right is a question; everyone in Charles Van Schaick's photograph appears to have confidence in the cornet player except the skeptical young man at lower right. In the curious sylvan scene above, a woodsman listens to the scratchy tones of a Graphophone—a hand-wound rig that did something less than justice to Sousa's marches, arias, devotional music, rural comedy and the flat voice of President McKinley.

COLLECTION OF EDITH LAFRANCIS

NATIONAL ARCHIVES

COLLECTION OF EDITH LAFRANCIS

It was the age of the horse. The most admired man in any small town was the dandy with a sporty rig and a pair of perfectly matched bays or blacks—spirited animals that performed like Arabian stallions when he showed them off. For the tradesman, a truly reliable horse was essential: he pulled the cart in all sorts of weather; he knew every stop along the delivery route and sensed when to start up again; he won friends and influenced customers; and, best of all, he was a splendid listener. Alvah and George Howes, itinerant photographers of Ashfield, Massachusetts, took the pictures opposite of the Grand Union Tea Company wagon and the sprinkling truck used to wet down dusty streets; the bakery and ice wagons directly below; and peddler William Mayer, who sold brooms, kettles, agate- and tin-ware, and notions in Hartford, Connecticut. Rural Free Delivery (opposite, left) moved by horse cart, and even a horse sometimes hitched a ride in a vehicle (bottom, left) drawn by a pair of dappled friends. We do not know who took these last two pictures.

COLLECTION OF EDITH LAFRANCIS

COLLECTION OF EDITH LAFRANCIS

DEPARTMENT OF PHOTOGRAPHY, OHIO STATE UNIVERSITY

COLLECTION OF EDITH LAFRANCIS

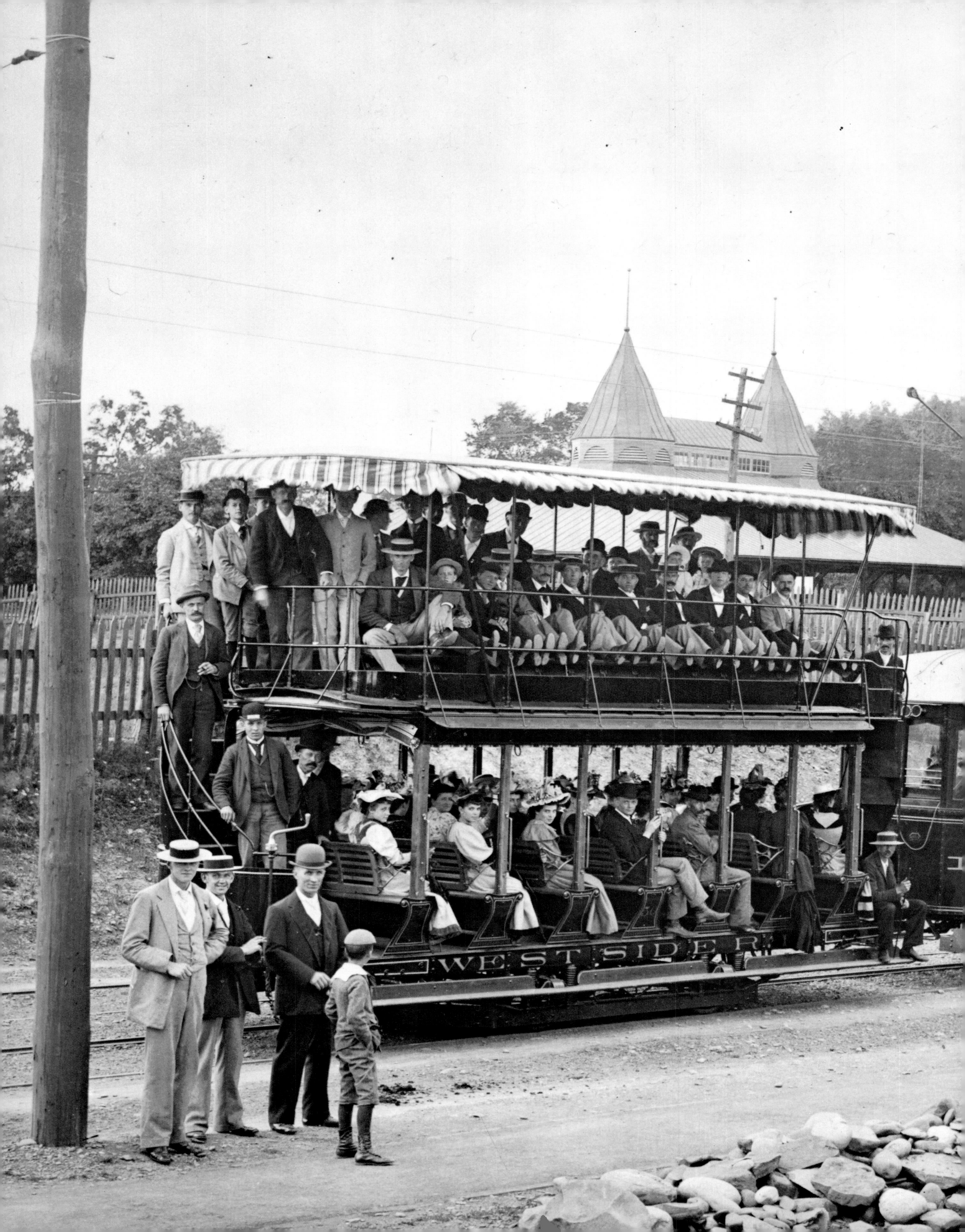
WEST SIDE R

COLLECTION OF STEPHEN D. MAGUIRE

Where you didn't go by horse, you usually went by trolley or interurban, and the traction companies were quick to see that one of the best ways to attract patronage was to provide fun and games at the end of the line. So the "car parks" came into being—amusement parks with ponds and rowboats, playgrounds and picnic facilities, dance pavilions and roller coasters—innocent pleasures for the lower and middle classes, and all for the price of a round-trip open trolley ride. An unknown photographer took the group at left, dressed to the nines, ready for an outing at Eldridge Park, near Elmira, New York, about 1900. The double-decker was a trailer, pulled by No. 19, an electric trolley. In later years, many of these double-decker trailers were motorized to enable them to operate independently, and later still, some were converted into single-deckers. In the photograph below, taken by the Howes brothers about 1905, a trolley crew is at work completing a section of the interurban line between Hartford, Connecticut, and Springfield, Massachusetts. Nothing equalled the sensation of riding a big, wooden interurban car that dusted along like the wind, swaying from side to side, its air horn shrieking at crossings, its windows open to catch the breezes and smells of summer. Since then we have enjoyed a great deal of "progress"—Rockefeller's oil fumes, Detroit's cramped automobiles, and everybody's disfiguring roads. Is travel as pleasant as in a buggy, or a sleigh, or the old open trolley?

COLLECTION OF EDITH LAFRANCIS

MUSEUM OF THE CITY OF NEW YORK

These stout hearts from Astoria made up Long Island's single hook-and-ladder company, photographed about 1888 by a man—or woman—known to us only by the Old Testament name of Baal.

The natty Phinney Hose Company volunteers below, well known for miles around for their precision drills, were the pride of Cooperstown, New York, when Arthur Telfer took their picture in 1871.

NEW YORK STATE HISTORICAL ASSOCIATION

NEW YORK STATE HISTORICAL ASSOCIATION

Nothing was dearer to the hearts of small-town Americans, or more certain to bring a shiver to their spines, than a good patriotic tableau. This electrifying example, put on by six young ladies of the Susan Fenimore Cooper Foundation, a Cooperstown orphanage, was also photographed by Telfer.

The Big City

Rural life in the latter half of the nineteenth century tended to preserve the face of an older America characterized by an abiding attachment to the land and a measured pace geared to the rhythm of the seasons. But meanwhile the rush of people from the farms to the cities, the thrust of urban building, industrial capitalism, and the incoming millions from overseas were shaping a future when we would be, for all our vast acreage, a nation of city dwellers.

Between 1815 and 1914 some thirty million people entered the United States from foreign lands, the greatest concentrated migration in recorded human history. Before the 1880's this flood of humanity was assimilated with comparative ease. The great majority of these newcomers came from the nations of northern and western Europe—the British Isles, Germany, Scandinavia—and they did not significantly alter the basic ethnic composition of the existing population. In addition, comparatively few except the Irish lingered in the ports of entry; instead most hurried westward to seek the land they had been denied in Europe. The growth of cities at this time stemmed largely from the nation's internal migration, triggered by industrialism.

After about 1885, however, the sources of immigration changed radically. Increasingly it was the peoples of eastern and southern Europe who filled the immigrant ships. In the last decade of the nineteenth century half a million Germans entered the United States, as opposed to three times that number in the previous decade; by contrast, in the first ten years of the twentieth century over two million Italians arrived, twice the total that had emigrated in the previous eighty years. This "new immigration" was not absorbed as easily into the American mainstream as was the old. With their alien ways and their alien tongues, the newcomers found a faint welcome or outright hostility in the land of opportunity. Few native Americans could then foresee the rise of a Fiorello La Guardia or a David Dubinsky or the steady mixing of European peoples into the mid-twentieth-century American. Nativists spoke bitterly of an "oozing leak of a sewer pipe into the crystal water of a well." In their overwhelming numbers (1,285,000 arrived in 1907, the peak year) the new immigrants piled up in the urban, industrialized areas of the East and Midwest.

"We cannot all live in cities," Horace Greeley had said long before, "yet nearly all seemed determined to do so." Alarmists trotted out Thomas Jefferson's warning of 1787. "When we get piled upon one another in large cities," Jefferson wrote, "we shall become as corrupt as in Europe, and go to eating one another as they do there." However seriously one might take Jefferson's prophecy, there was no question that America's greatest cities were staggering under the twin impacts of the new immigration and industrialization. "A map of the city, colored to designate nationalities," Jacob Riis wrote of New York in 1890, "would show more stripes than on the skin of a zebra, and more colors than any rainbow. The city on such a map would fall into two great halves, green for the Irish prevailing in the West Side tenement districts, and blue for the Germans on the East Side. But intermingled with these ground colors would be an odd variety of tints that would give the whole the appearance of an extraordinary crazy-quilt." In this crazy-quilt urban world all the problems that plague our cities today—slums, overloaded mass transport, overburdened police and fire and health services, inadequate public funds, and the rest—struck deep roots and flourished.

The phenomenon of the mushrooming city was as obvious to contemporaries as it is to us in retrospect, and photographers were fully alert to the ongoing drama. Represented on the following pages are some of the great names in photography; artists like Mathew Brady, Eadweard Muybridge (famous for his pioneering studies of animals and humans in motion), the reformer Lewis Hine, the remarkable Alice Austen. Also stalking the broad avenues and close slums was a legion of unsung photographers who in the course of their daily labors created masterpieces. We know little about the people in the pictures that follow. The daring, neatly dressed young man on the opposite page, for example, is unidentified; we know only that the caption on this 1905 stereo says he is perched "on a slender support eighteen stories above the pavement of Fifth Avenue." But known or unknown, he and his fellows were there, and in their pictures we see modern-day America emerging literally before our eyes.

COLLECTION OF DR. PHILIP BATCHELDER

Jutting up in the foreground is an iron finial on the tower of Hopkins' mansion, site of today's Mark Hopkins Hotel—the panorama, you could say, was made from "the Top of the Mark." The photographer was Eadweard Muybridge (the eccentric spelling was his own idea of the Saxon rendering of plain Edward Muggeridge). Muybridge set up twelve cameras to record the scene full circle; we reproduce four of the plates here. Soon to rise on the hillock in the foreground was the one-and-a-half-million-dollar Flood mansion; sole Nob Hill survivor of the 1906 fire, it is now The Pacific-Union Club. The large mansard-roofed house was that of James Ben Ali Haggin, a descendant of Christianized Turks and a prominent attorney. Two houses to the right lived the president of the Wells Fargo Bank, Lloyd Tevis.

WELLS FARGO BANK HISTORY ROOM

If railroad nabob Mark Hopkins had lived to see his palatial Nob Hill mansion completed, he would have commanded this panoramic view of San Francisco, shown here in January, 1877, from its roof. In the foreground of the first panel is California Street, still building, as the rubble testifies. The white marble mansion belonged to David Colton, a lesser breed of rail magnate known as "the One Half of the Big Four and One Half." Collis P. Huntington would buy it after Colton's death in 1878. Next door lived yet another railway king, Charles Crocker, a man few dared to cross: when his neighbor, an undertaker named Yung, refused to sell out to him, Crocker surrounded Yung's house on three sides with a gigantic forty-foot spite fence (which here appears to be in Colton's back yard rather than Crocker's).

The Rise and Fall of a City

In Gold Rush days, and just after, San Francisco was a crude, man's town. These lads are clowning with a storekeeper's whiskey and hoops for ladies' skirts, about 1855. Yet only a generation later this miner's and sailor's city had become the great metropolis in the foldout under these pages. Then, as we see on pages 236-237, a terrible disaster struck.

BANCROFT LIBRARY

LIBRARY OF CONGRESS

Shortly after 5:00 A.M. on April 18, 1906, San Francisco photographer Arnold Genthe was startled awake. "The whole house was creaking and shaking, the chandelier was swinging like a pendulum, and I felt as if I were on a ship tossed about by a rough sea," Genthe wrote later. The earthquake drove people from their homes by the thousands. "The streets presented a weird appearance," he recalled; "men in pajamas . . . and dinner coats, women scantily dressed with evening wraps hastily thrown over them." In the lobby of the St. Francis Hotel, Genthe came upon Enrico Caruso, whom he had seen perform the night before in Carmen. *"'Ell of a place! 'Ell of a place!" Caruso muttered. "I never come back here." Fires sprang up everywhere, with firemen helpless to contain them because the quake had shattered the water mains. For seventy-two hours the heart of the city burned. The militia dynamited whole blocks to act as firebreaks. Genthe took the picture at left, as two young women incongruously clowned for him, from the top of one of the city's hills. "Ten square miles lay devastated with hardly a building intact," he wrote. Over 650 were dead, a quarter million were homeless, and property losses topped half a billion dollars. The picture above, by the firm of H. C. White & Co., shows ruined Chinatown. In the background on Nob Hill are the granite walls of the new Fairmont Hotel, its interior a total loss. Fire and other disasters have long been the lot of city dwellers, but San Francisco's agony was perhaps the greatest an American city had ever experienced. Yet it rose again fast enough to stage the great Panama-Pacific Exposition only nine years later.*

CALIFORNIA PALACE OF THE LEGION OF HONOR

When building a capital city over which the flag will long wave, haste is unseemly. Witness these examples from Washington, D.C. Below, one of the noble Grecian columns fronting the north wing of the Treasury is inched into place in 1867. The Treasury took thirty-three years to complete, but we are pleased to report that Ulysses S. Grant's inaugural ball went off without a hitch in the cash room of the north wing only eighteen months after this picture was taken; by whom, no one knows. Construction of the Washington Monument dragged on for thirty-six years; Mathew Brady showed it (opposite) in 1879, when it had reached just over 150 feet. "It has the aspect of a factory chimney with the top broken off," Mark Twain remarked, "tired pigs dozing in the holy calm of its protecting shadow." The Army Engineers took over and raised it to its height of 555 feet in five years.

CHICAGO HISTORICAL SOCIETY

"Mechanical ingenuity engages a greater number of minds in the United States than in any other nation," observed the English physicist John Tyndall in 1872, the year this photograph was taken, by an unknown but skillful hand. The scene is the Brooklyn tower of the mighty Brooklyn Bridge, then in its fourth year of construction. In 1869 the celebrated engineer John A. Roebling devised a plan to vault New York's East River, joining the nation's first and third largest cities with a suspension bridge. Before construction began, however, Roebling was fatally injured. The job was completed by his son, Washington, who was himself crippled for life by an attack of the "bends" while working in a caisson below the river.

OVERLEAF: *The "eighth wonder of the world," completed in 1883, looked like this from the Brooklyn side about 1900. The glass plate, now slightly battered, is the work of the Wittemann Brothers, who specialized in post cards and souvenir views. These massive Gothic towers and spidery cables have long inspired poets and artists; to immigrant Joseph Stella, who painted it many times, the Brooklyn Bridge symbolized "the joyful, daring endeavor of the American civilization."*

LIBRARY OF CONGRESS, WITTEMANN COLLECTION

CULVER PICTURES

FRANKLI
17
WILLIAM McQUADE.
BONDED WAREHOUSE LIQUORS
VALENTINE SCHMITT.
No. 11
IMPORTER OF RHINE WINES.
WILLIAM E. SMITH.
VALENTINE, BERGEN & CO.

CULVER PICTURES

While the Brooklyn Bridge took shape, New Yorkers were introduced to the ubiquitous elevated railroad. A New Jersey photographer named J. Reid posed this tableau on the Third Avenue El in the 1880's: the passengers wait impatiently for the conductor, lordly in wing collar, to give the all clear.

The cars boasted oak and mahogany panelwork and Axminster carpeting, and cost a dime (later a nickel) to ride. Steam locomotives blackened many a wash and fired many an awning before the turn of the century, when the lines were electrified. The Third Avenue El, last of its breed, expired in 1955.

LIBRARY OF CONGRESS

Two unidentified turn-of-the-century photographers paid tribute to two landmarks in the history of American architecture. Above, the Flatiron Building rises in New York in 1901. Scoffers stood at a safe distance to watch it crumble at the first high wind, betting that the debris would scatter as far as Madison Avenue. The property, at Broadway and Fifth Avenue, was known as a "stingy piece of pie" and the "cowcatcher," but its owner, Amos R. Eno, easily bore the jibes. The land was bought in 1857 for $32,000, produced millions in rentals, and was sold by his heirs for $690,000 in 1899. At the windy prow of the building loungers gathered to watch the ladies try to manage their skirts. "Hanging about this particular spot," wrote an English visitor in a pre-miniskirt era, "soon became a recognized and punishable offense." The splendid hole in the ground at right is Pennsylvania Station under construction in 1908. Architect Stanford White took as his model such structures as the Baths of Caracalla, and the 150-foot-high waiting room eclipsed all previous American terminals. Its destruction in 1966 is too painful to recount.

LIBRARY OF CONGRESS, DETROIT PUBLISHING COMPANY COLLECTION

MACY'S
IRON WORKS

BOTH: COLLECTION OF ANDREW SPANO

This frowning countenance—this fearsome, *frowning countenance—is the face of the Statue of Liberty, photographed at Bedloe's Island in New York Harbor in 1885. Assembled and crowned and in place, we admit, she looks better. The name of the photographer of both pictures has, alas, disappeared.*

Miss Liberty's head of hammered sheet copper, here seen inside out, was welded over this iron framework, designed by Gustave Eiffel, who built the Paris tower. The huge figure, enlarged from a model by Auguste Bartholdi, stands 151 feet high, a good fifty feet higher than the Colossus of Rhodes.

JAMES WADSWORT
JAMES W. WADSWORTH.

STATEN ISLAND HISTORICAL SOCIETY

"I lift my lamp beside the golden door," reads the final line of Emma Lazarus' poem inscribed on the base of the Statue of Liberty. In the 1880's the golden door to America for most immigrants opened at Castle Garden, at the tip of Lower Manhattan. The flood tide of newcomers, however, rendered Castle Garden wholly inadequate, and a new immigration center was opened on Ellis Island, out in the harbor, in 1892. The immigrants were delivered there by barge from the steamship piers, and there they were registered, questioned, and given health examinations. Indigents, lunatics, convicted criminals; all were barred. An 1891 law had also barred polygamists and "persons suffering from a loathsome contagious disease." Those with lesser diseases were quarantined in hospitals, one of which was on Staten Island. This picture by Alice Austen shows the quarantine paddle-wheeler James W. Wadsworth *in the 1890's. From the dress of the passengers we can assume that they have been released from quarantine and are at last about to enter the golden door.*

OVERLEAF: *What the majority of immigrants faced after the mid-1880's is captured in Warren Dickerson's view of Hester Street on the Lower East Side of New York at the turn of the century. The people of Hester Street were mostly Russian Jews, and the area was noted for its food peddlers, in evidence here, and for producing trimmings for the garment trade; M. Horowitz (at right center), for example, was a trimmer. One newcomer, Anzia Yezierska, described her first impressions as a young girl freshly arrived from Russia: "Between buildings that loomed like mountains we struggled with our bundles . . . through the swarming streets of the Ghetto. . . . I looked about the narrow streets of squeezed-in stores and houses, ragged clothes, dirty bedding oozing out of the windows, ash-cans and garbage cans cluttering the sidewalks. A vague sadness pressed down my heart, the first doubt of America. . . . I looked out into the alley below, and saw pale-faced children scrambling in the gutter. 'Where is America?' cried my heart." America, it turned out, was uptown, and there, propelled by hard work, study, and thrift, the Jews flocked. Behind them the houses gradually came down, and all that one sees in this picture is now replaced by faceless modern apartment buildings.*

LOS ANGELES COUNTY MUSEUM OF NATURAL HISTORY

23
BATHS
PLUNGE
BATHS
VAPOR & SWIM BATH.

19 . M. HOROWITZ . 19

PICNIC
ELECTRICAL CABLE SPLICERS HELPERS
SAT. EVE. JULY 25
AMERICAN EXPRESS
RELAUNDERED

The ultimate symbol of America's burgeoning big cities at the turn of the century was not the soaring skyscraper or the graceful bridge or the marble mansion, but rather the New York tenement, the befouled, crowded, airless structure that was home to ever-increasing numbers of people. This back-yard scene in New York is also the work of Warren Dickerson. In How the Other Half Lives*, a pioneering study of New York's slums, the photographer and reformer Jacob Riis described a tenement of the eighties: "The hall is dark, and you might stumble over the children pitching pennies back there. Not that it would hurt them; kicks and cuffs are their daily diet.... All the fresh air that ever enters these stairs comes from the hall door that is forever slamming, and from the windows of dark bedrooms that in turn receive from the stairs their sole supply of the elements God meant to be free. The sinks are in the hallway, that all the tenants may have access—and all be poisoned alike by their summer stenches...."*

LOS ANGELES COUNTY MUSEUM OF NATURAL HISTORY

The photographs below of the organ-grinder and the newsgirl are the work of Alice Austen, who came into Manhattan from rural Staten Island to take them in 1896. The picture at lower left, by an unknown New Orleans photographer, shows a scissors-grinder at about the same period. He is a natty sort, shoes shined, pencil and order book at the ready; with the grinding machine carried on his shoulder, the hard hat was a necessity. By 1890, Harper's Weekly *tells us, the traditional Italian organ-grinder was in decline, owing largely to laws against solicitation by costumed monkeys. The pretty newsgirl, peddling her papers outside the Forty-Second Street ferry terminal, was a rarity; the 1900 census showed a proportion of one hundred newsboys to one newsgirl. The stalwarts at right posed for Miss Austen against a backdrop of the Sixth Avenue El. The patrolman was part of a police force of 4,156 who protected a population of two million. The White Wing belonged to the well-run Department of Street Cleaning, which seventeen days after this picture was taken held its first parade. The sweepers and shovellers proudly marched two thousand strong, with 750 horses pulling carts and machines. But we had not conquered snow (see next page), nor have we entirely yet.*

LIBRARY OF CONGRESS

STATEN ISLAND HISTORICAL SOCIETY

COLLECTION OF OLIVER JENSEN

STATEN ISLAND HISTORICAL SOCIETY

CHICAGO HISTORICAL SOCIETY

A Chicago newspaper photographer, now unhappily anonymous, took the photograph above of a horse-drawn snowplow struggling along Michigan Avenue, in a record-setting blizzard of 1908.

Up until the First World War the noble horse provided most of the motive power for most services needed by city dwellers. These sharply contrasting scenes were taken in St. Louis. Charles Trefts' picture below memorializes the pride of the city's fire department, in breathtaking action about 1900. Listen to one J. Thomas Scharf describe the drama of the smoke-eaters: "At the first stroke of the signal-box the firemen spring from their places, rush to the horses, and in another moment the harness is on, and the intelligent animals . . . stalk unbidden to the apparatus. The match is applied, and in another instant they are on their way. Nothing is heard but the rumbling of the wheels . . . the quick step of the horses, and the occasional sharp whistle which is given en route. . . ." The grim picture at right, taken by Charles C. Holt in 1913, shows a "dead animal" wagon. Working horses died by the score in St. Louis' summer heat; that year alone the toll exceeded four thousand.

OVERLEAF: *Lewis W. Hine is one of the great names in the history of documentary photography. He produced notable picture studies of the human drama of Ellis Island and of the dignity of industrial workers; his series on child labor and the exploited women of the sweatshops was instrumental in achieving reform legislation. This picture, from a group entitled "The Slum Dwellers," shows part of the so-called alley slums of Washington, D.C., in 1908. Into one of these crumbling brick and frame houses behind Dupont Circle as many as thirty Negro families were crammed, sharing one outside water tap and one fetid privy. This blight was removed only after World War II.*

GEORGE EASTMAN HOUSE COLLECTION

STATE HISTORICAL SOCIETY OF MISSOURI, CHARLES TREFTS COLLECTION

COLLECTION OF DICK LEMEN

POSITIVELY
NO ADMITTANCE
WITHOUT PASS

CULVER PICTURES

When Cornelius Vanderbilt II, grandson of the old Commodore, decided to build in New York City, he chose as his architect George B. Post, protégé of Richard Morris Hunt, builder to the Four Hundred. The result (left), recorded by an unknown photographer, was a notable tourist attraction. The Château de Blois, as it was called, occupied the block on Fifth Avenue between Fifty-seventh and Fifty-eighth Streets, now the site of that fancy dry-goods emporium, Bergdorf Goodman. It was built of red brick trimmed in grey limestone, and owed its inspiration to the chateaux of the Loire Valley. This is the Fifty-seventh Street, or "everyday," entrance, as it neared completion in 1881. Among the house staff of thirty, the New York Herald *reported, was a platoon of parlor maids who devoted the three hours from six to nine every morning to sweeping, dusting, and polishing the drawing room and downstairs halls. The Vanderbilts had no corner on the Good Life; all the well-to-do did well indeed in the days before the income tax reared its ugly head. Chicago Society, depicted below, found a tallyho ideal for viewing the races. The lady at the left is Mrs. Arthur Caton, later Marshall Field's second wife. Next comes Franklin MacVeagh, very big in wholesale groceries, and next to him is Mrs. Arthur Meeker, of the South Side Meekers.*

OVERLEAF: *The great bridges and monumental buildings, the glittering mansions and abysmal slums, were not the whole story of the American city in its youth; it is appropriate, in closing our chapter, to pay tribute to the city's pleasures and excitements as well. Consider Main Street, Buffalo, New York, on Labor Day in 1905. It is all here—ladies in holiday finery, gentlemen in straw boaters, trolley cars in stately procession, horse-drawn gigs, bicycles; even an ice-cream parlor.*

LIBRARY OF CONGRESS, DETROIT PUBLISHING COMPANY COLLECTION

CHICAGO HISTORICAL SOCIETY

THE
RIENZI
HOTEL

444
SUGAR BOWL.
WESTERN
SAVINGS BANK OF BUFFALO
CURTIS SIGNS
De La FRANIER
GLASSWARE
KING.
COURT ST.
THEATRE
FLOOR FOR RENT
442
ROTHSCHILD'S
PAWN SHOP
ROTHSCHILD'S
PAWN SHOP
1/2
DR. LAWTON
DENTIST
LAWTON
DENTAL PARLORS
C.P. STEIN Jr. TAILOR
DENTIST
D. LEVIN 442
ICE CREAM PARLOR
446 DRY GOODS

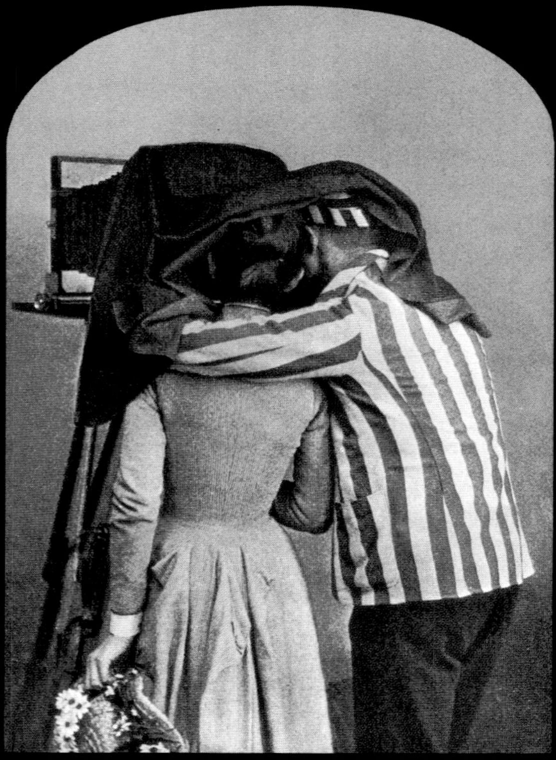

444
SUGAR BOWL.
WESTERN SAVINGS BANK OF BUFFALO
KING.
COURT ST. THEATRE
CURTIS SIGNS
GLASSWARE
De La FRANIER
442
ROTHSCHILD'S PAWN SHOP.
THE OLD RELIABLE ROTHSCHILD'S PAWN SHOP
C.P. STEIN JR. TAILOR.
DR. LAWTON DENTIST
DENTAL PARLORS.
D. LEVIN 442
ICE CREAM PARLOR.
446 DRY GOODS

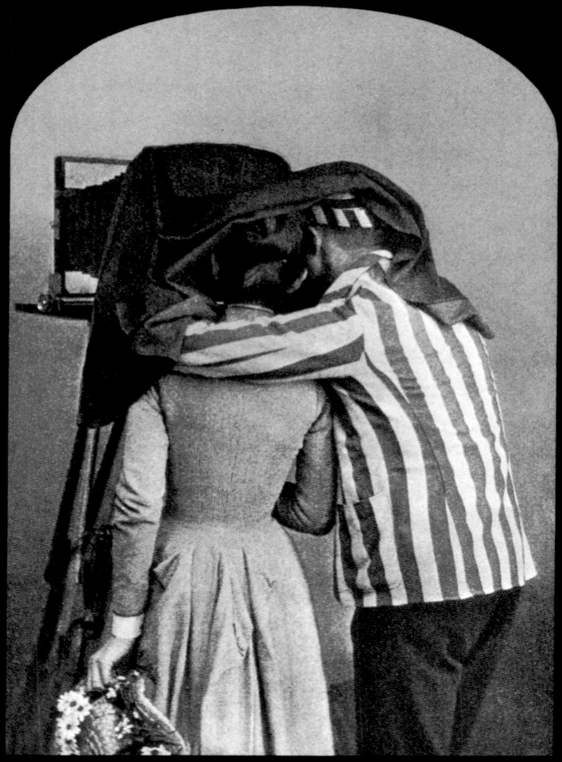

Patterns of Life

In America as in the world at large—but somehow more swiftly here—fashions and styles and manners change, intents and purposes shift, new ideas are discovered only to be swept aside by still newer ones, many of which turn out to be the old ones previously tried and forgotten. One century's yeomanry is another's gentry, and vice versa. We call this life, and we alternately bless and curse it, invariably waste it, but seldom regret it.

To each human being the cycle seems unique, and nearly all of us have an instinct for having it recorded. Fortunately, ever since photography was invented there seems to have been, in even the smallest American town, someone who could operate a camera with a fair—and often a better-than-fair—degree of proficiency. These amateur and professional graphic historians recorded such great revolutionary changes in America as the westward migration, the transportation explosion, the decline of the farm, and the growth of the city. But they also turned their lenses on the ordinary life cycle of the ordinary American, and when we look back at *those* photographs, we perceive another revolution just as startling and ultimately as meaningful.

The world our grandparents knew was much more sharply compartmented than our own. There were large areas—not just the saloon and the barbershop but politics, business, and the professions—exclusively reserved for men. There were others—the kitchen, of course, but also the world of fashion and, for the most part, the realm of "culture"—that were the preserve of women. An American of the eighties or nineties suddenly reincarnated in the 1960's would of course be astounded by one-hundred-story skyscrapers and twelve-hundred-mile-an-hour jet airplanes; but these are, after all, only extensions of technological innovations whose beginnings, at least, he glimpsed. He would not be at all prepared, on the other hand, for the scenes that would greet him in a business office, a cocktail lounge, or a polling place. What broke down so completely the barriers between the separate worlds of men and women? How did American society become so homogenized?

And what would he think of our children? In his day youngsters were seen but not heard (nor were they supposed to hear—little pitchers had big ears). Perhaps today's greater concern with the child's emotional and intellectual growth, the freer give and take within the family circle, and the respect, indeed almost the deference, accorded the opinions of the young are improvements over the world Grandpa knew. Perhaps. But he would not think so: for one thing, no longer would his advanced years and broad experience of life count for much. Where once the elderly were revered they are now merely tolerated, ever less patiently. Modern America squanders the wisdom of the aged.

That is one reason we have published the moving portrait of Walt Whitman with two little moppets on pages 318-319. Another reason has to do with the artistry of George Collins Cox, whose work is largely forgotten today but who, at the turn of the century, was established as one of the nation's foremost portrait photographers. Between 1883, when he moved his studio from New Jersey to Greenwich Village, and his death in 1903, a stream of Presidents, First Ladies, bishops, generals, admirals, politicians, and other *hochwohlgeborene* of the professions, the theatre, and the arts made their way to his door.

While Cox was probing for soul in the great, other imaginative photographers took their equipment and their concerns out into the streets, into the public baths of the poor and the plush banquet rooms of the rich, into the forest primeval or the forest despoiled, onto construction sites, into the classrooms of the affluent or the impoverished, into salons and saloons and bagnios, into the theatre and the subway. Occasionally one of them, like Charles Schenk, even parted the draperies of convention and rediscovered the human body. Life was what these early photographers focused on, and if some of them did not trouble to leave us enough caption information, perhaps it was because they felt that their pictures spoke for themselves.

Consider the dapper photographer in the striped blazer, opposite, who has obviously discovered a new use for the dark cloth on his camera. We have no way of knowing what he and his girl friend are looking at on the ground glass, but it must have been quite a scene!

A Man's World

Despite the alarming gains made by the feminist movement between the Civil War and World War I, the nineteenth century, as our subtitle indicates, still very much belonged to the male animal. Girls were taught to read, of course, and to do simple arithmetic, but it was the men who were sent to college. Father's word was more equal than Mother's in the home, which was pretty much where the women were expected to stay. On the job, at the office, in the professions, men predominated. After the work was done, men continued to enjoy an exclusiveness that is simply incomprehensible to the current generation. Men associated with each other, and were less uxorious than today. Saloons were off-limits to women; so were such sacrosanct emporiums as the cigar store and especially the barbershop. But mainly there was work. Medieval Christianity created the concept that honest labor is a service to God, and the Protestant Reformation added a profit incentive, but the work ethic really came to full flower during the settlement of the United States. And why not? Everywhere there were things to do, things to build, things to create. America was unlimited opportunity, and the greatest opportunity of all was the chance to work. And so the American workman came into being—rough and proud and contemptuous of traditional divisions of labor, equal to any challenge. Best of all, this artisan, liberated from long-standing convention, not yet hemmed in by mid-twentieth-century unionism, could improvise: if the old method didn't work, he tried another; if the traditional tool was inadequate, he invented another. In the process he levelled forests, erected cities, built highways, laid railroads, burrowed through mountains, drained swamps, changed the course of rivers. Occasionally the American workman put down his adze and his trowel to pose before a lens. If he happened to be working in western Massachusetts around the turn of the century, as did the construction men at right, the chances were that he would stare into a camera carried by two itinerant photographers, Alvah and George Howes of Ashfield. The brothers Howes asked little of their subjects except that they remain stationary; they left us even less information about the results. Even so, this photograph—suffused with the quiet, confident strength of workers united, not separated, by their skills—speaks volumes about the character and mettle of the men who built this nation.

OVERLEAF: *By 1900, barbed wire and the railroads had put an end to that most romantic aspect of ranching, the overland cattle drive to market; yet for years the routine of ranch operation remained cruelly arduous. When an unseasonable blizzard threatened the herd, the cowhands worked night and day in frozen saddles to lead the helpless yearlings to sheltered meadows. This unusual panorama was taken early in this century in Wyoming, on the Pitchfork Ranch, owned by Charles J. Belden, who until his death in 1966 was known as the country's best photographer of the cowboy.*

CHARLES J. BELDEN ESTATE

COLLECTION OF EDITH LAFRANCIS

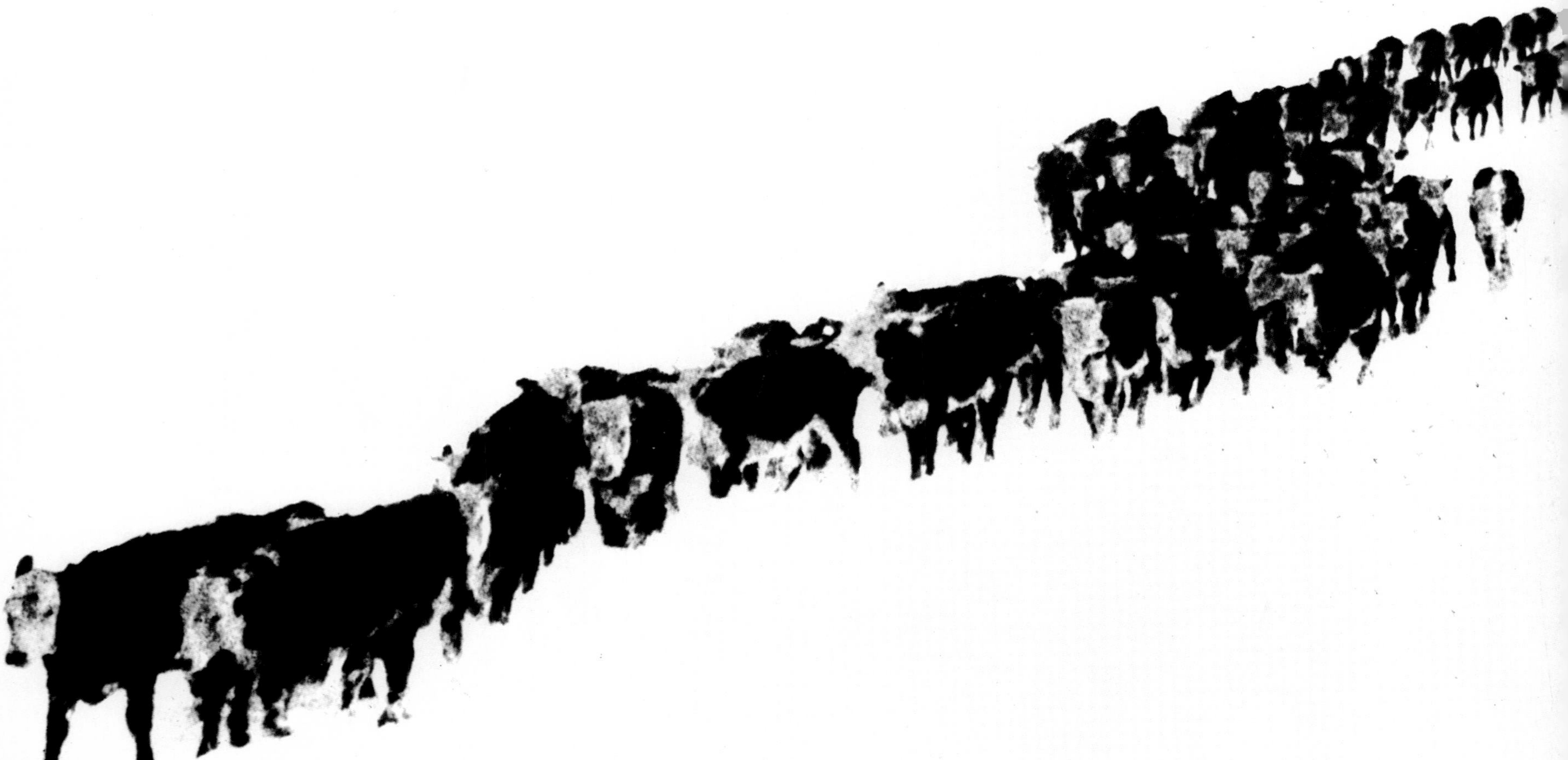

HISTORY OF PHOTOGRAPHY COLLECTION, SMITHSONIAN INSTITUTION

Normally, George Collins Cox preferred to photograph his illustrious subjects in his studio, but when larger-than-life characters like Henry Hobson Richardson (opposite) and William Merritt Chase (below) came along, Cox was more than willing to pack up his bulky equipment and go to them. Richardson was the architect and railroad station builder chiefly responsible for starting in 1872 the Romanesque revival that still bears his name; so popular was the style that crude imitations of his design for Trinity Church in Boston were being produced across the nation even before the church was finished in 1877. Richardson's fascination with things medieval extended to the interior of his New York home, where he affected the monastic dress shown by Cox's camera. Chase was eccentric in a different way. Having established his reputation as a painter in Europe, he returned in 1878 to become a teacher at the Art Students League and one of the leaders of the revolt against the traditional conventions of the academy. His studio, lavishly decorated with bibelots and curios and paintings from all over the world, was for seventeen years a Mecca for New York artists.

OVERLEAF: *While some men built and created, others destroyed in a never-ending search for raw materials with which to erect a nation. The forests went first, felled by a hardy band of men to whom even the giant redwood was merely a larger challenge. The camera-carrying Boswell of the loggers of the Pacific Northwest was an itinerant photographer named Darius Kinsey, who convinced the lumbermen that "you aren't a logger until you own a dollar watch and have your picture taken with a tree." In fifty years of making men loggers, he assembled a splendid record of lumbering's prime.*

CULVER PICTURES

MUSEUM OF THE CITY OF NEW YORK

COLLECTION OF OLIVER JENSEN

The world of chemistry was still limited enough to be covered in three years when this happy quartet graduated from Yale in 1880. Third from left is the author's grandfather, Martin E. Jensen. There is no record as to just whose experiment has overflowed all over the bottom step.

OVERLEAF: *The young stenographer in this great office scene of 1907 was but the vanguard of a revolution that has triumphed. She earned about six to eight dollars a week, and was advised to keep her skirts three inches off the floor, or full length if the premises happened to be carpeted.*
THE BYRON COLLECTION, MUSEUM OF THE CITY OF NEW YORK

PARIS
LONDON
BERLIN

Santos Sotello
Robbed Stages in Kern and Los Angeles counties in 1877

Dick Fellows
Sent to Folsom State Prison April 1882 for life

Louis L Cole
Confidence Man

Wm Barber
Robbed Yreka Stage July 18 1877 with Joe Blanchard who was Killed in Arresting

John Weisenstine
Arrested for Hills Ferry Stage robbery of April 27" 1882

Joe Brown
Robbed Shasta Stage in 1877 with Dave Tye and Tom Brown

Geo Adams
Robbed Stage from Nerhall to Soledad alone Dec. 3" 1879

Charlie Dorsey "Alias" Thorn
One of the Cummings Murderers, Mare's Flat Stage Sept. 1st 1879 Nevada Co.

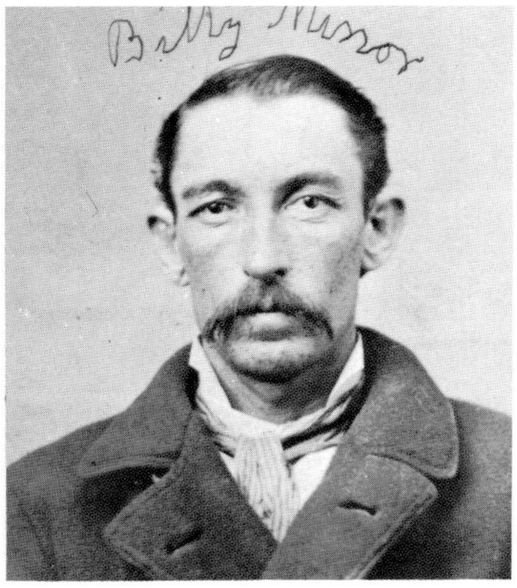

W. A. Miner
Robbed San Andreas Stage Jan. 23-1871 in Company with Alkali Jim & Chas Cooper

Sam Lansing
While acting as Cashier of Kern Co Bank stole $28.000 confessed & returned the money

Unlike the Canadian Mounties, Wells Fargo did not always get its man. But when those pioneer express agents did run a desperado to earth, they made sure to record his image—alive or, in the instance of Brazleton below, very dead. These photographs, collected by company agents between 1864 and 1887 and annotated in a nice old hand, are part of a dilapidated little album in the History Room of the Wells Fargo Bank in San Francisco. In those days there were still a few occupations for men only, and the ninety-five men thus enshrined shared one common accomplishment: they had all robbed Wells Fargo, usually by gaining access to the strongbox kept under the driver's seat of a rumbling Concord stage. Some were bloodthirsty killers, who shot first and resisted answering questions later; others were rank amateurs in search of a grubstake. The exact purpose of this album is not known, although it would appear to be a private rogues' gallery, a crime-fighting use of the camera which the law was quick to seize upon.

Jim Driscoll
Robbed Stage from Fiddletown to Sacramento in 1864

H. C. Paige
Opened the box with Keys on Pendleton Stage July 10" 1880 and Stole $2456 00

Brazleton
Robbed four or five Stages in Arizona during the year 1878 and 1879 was Killed in arresting

ALL: WELLS FARGO BANK HISTORY ROOM

ALL: PENNELL COLLECTION, UNIVERSITY OF KANSAS

In the early 1900's no women were permitted or wanted in John Gartner's Cigar Store, Rudy Sohn's Barber Shop, or the Horseshoe Saloon, in Junction City, Kansas. Haircuts were still a quarter, and the Saturday shave in preparation for church was bristly custom; each man had

his own brand of tobacco or cut plug and a clerk who remembered; and the saloon served nothing stronger than beer because Kansas had adopted prohibition in 1880. It is all changed now, but the husky atmosphere of these masculine enclaves lives on in J. J. Pennell's photographs.

LIBRARY OF CONGRESS, CURRIER COLLECTION

THE BYRON COLLECTION, MUSEUM OF THE CITY OF NEW YORK

The United States, to its eternal good fortune, has always had a large middle class, but the very phrase implies the concurrent existence of wealth and poverty. At no time in our history was the distance between the two as great as in those otherwise good old days at the turn of the century, when some of the urban poor could be periodically disinfected on an assembly-line basis while merry elements of the urban rich might be living very high only a few streets away. Observe, for a minute, the contrast. The Byron Company, a famous family photographic firm, recorded the vine-leaved festivities at the fin de siècle *dinner that New York* Mirror *editor-publisher Harrison Grey Fiske, seated on the right of the white-bearded gentleman, either gave or attended as guest of honor. Charles Currier was responsible for searing the public awareness with his reportorial treatment above of derelicts bathing at the Wayfarer's Lodge in Boston. Thousands annually passed through this sterile but scarcely homelike facility, which offered a clean bed and a hot meal in return for labor on the Lodge's woodpile.*

CULVER PICTURES

The Puritans hated sports, which they associated with such other moral pitfalls as idleness and pleasure, and this attitude lingered on into the mid-nineteenth century. Respectable sports appeared in the years following the Civil War, so that the beginnings of modern baseball and football, of golf and tennis, of track and crew, occurred in the age of photography. Lawn tennis was introduced into the United States in 1874 by Miss Mary Outerbridge of Staten Island, New York. She had learned the game in Bermuda, and brought back a full set of equipment. The game appealed immediately to the upper classes, especially because both sexes might play it, like croquet and (later on) bicycling. The dress of the unidentified young man at left gives a glimpse of what the game was like. Men wore stiff shirts, and sporty types wore striped blazers, but no gentleman would play in his shirt sleeves. Behold, also, those shoes. In the scene below we have the Yale freshman crew in 1885; their jerseys proclaim the year they will graduate. The man with the handlebar mustache, sitting at No. 5 oar, center, is the captain, William Herbert Corbin, nicknamed "Pa" because he was twenty-one years old when he entered Yale. He twice rowed in victories over Harvard varsity crews at New London, Connecticut, in the oldest intercollegiate athletic event in the country, established in 1852. But Pa really shone in football; he was the captain of the famed varsity team which in 1888 beat Wesleyan 105-0, then went on to total a fantastic 698 points for the season—while thirteen opponents failed to score at all. Pa never played a losing game for Yale, which could, Lord knows, use him now.

STERLING MEMORIAL LIBRARY, YALE UNIVERSITY

STATE HISTORICAL SOCIETY OF WISCONSIN

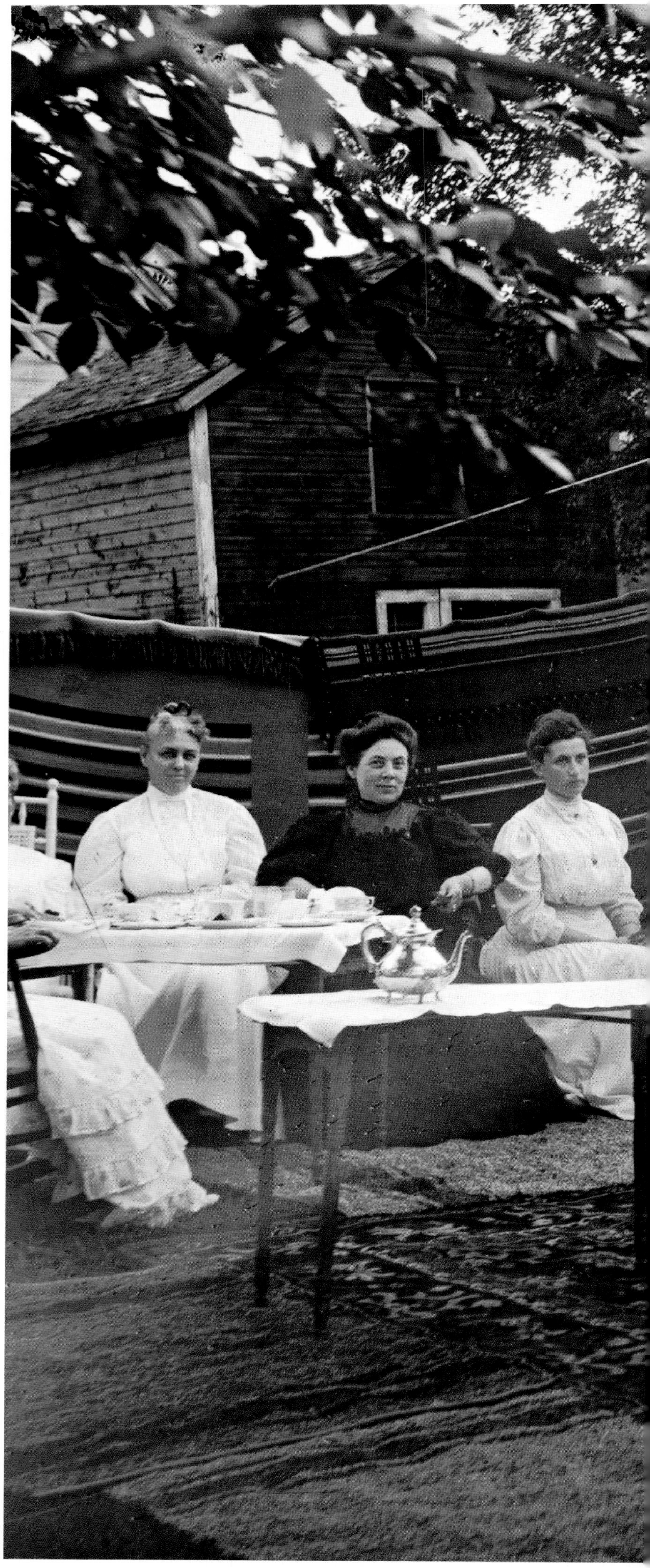

A Woman's Place

It is almost impossible to imagine a scene like this, even allowing for a change in dress, in the United States of today. The company would probably be mixed, the tea, cookies, and lemonade in most places would certainly be supplemented if not supplanted by cocktails. The older ladies of Black River Falls, Wisconsin, met regularly at each other's houses for a bit of tea, sewing, and gossip. In 1905 Charles Van Schaick caught his wife Ida (standing, in a polka-dot dress) playing hostess at such a session, called a "Kensington," in the garden behind their home. The rugs on the line were probably hung out as a windbreak, as it was early spring. The life of ordinary men in America has changed very little in the past century, compared with the vast alterations in the circumstances of women. In that sense, the pictures on the next few pages border on the unbelievable. Rich women lived relatively idle lives on their "pedestals," while poor ones knew, as the jingle says, that woman's work is never done. Poised variously between the extremes, those of the middle class were hedged about by a propriety even more restrictive than their formidable undergarments. "Good" women could easily be told from "bad" women in that pre-Freudian time. Woman's rightful place was in the home; save for a few disruptive advocates of women's rights, no one felt that women, much less ladies, belonged in the political, economic, or intellectual worlds. In sharp, clear old pictures like these you can almost lean in and touch the people; yet it would be easier, from a standpoint of sociological distance, to touch the moon.

Informality had no place in the social world that flourished in America before the First World War, and these ladies at a 1909 Long Island garden party certainly make that point. If one wanted to enjoy the out-of-doors fashionably it was de rigueur *to wear a large hat, gloves, a high collar, and perhaps a veil. There can be no question but that this gathering was fashionable, for some of New York's most glittering names were present. On the left is Mrs. Oren Root, niece by marriage of Elihu Root, Theodore Roosevelt's Secretary of State. Third from the left is Mrs. William K. Vanderbilt, the former Ann Harriman of the railroad Harrimans, who was probably the hostess. (The Vanderbilts were also railroaders: the old Commodore, W. K.'s grandfather, had collected a hundred million dollars from the New York Central.) Ann was W. K.'s second wife; his first had been the formidable social leader, Alva Vanderbilt, who divorced him and later married Oliver Hazard Perry Belmont. On the far right is Mrs. Charles Dana Gibson, wife of the famous creator of the Gibson Girl and sister of the acerbic Lady Astor.*

CULVER PICTURES

*There was one issue that made society ladies unbend—women's rights. The suffragettes below, photographed by George Grantham Bain as they solicited funds for the Cause on a New York sidewalk in 1913, might well have attended the party with the ladies opposite. From the time the women's suffrage movement began just before the Civil War until the Nineteenth Amendment gave women the vote in 1920, many of America's grandest dames were soldiers in the suffragettes' army. After all, it was Mrs. Oliver H. P. Belmont herself who made what is perhaps the most famous feminist remark in history: "Brace up, my dear. Just pray to God—*She *will help you." The movement, as the grinning face of the man on the left attests, was always a ready target for masculine mirth. Strong-minded as she was, the suffragette could ignore the jibes, but the more perceptive of her daughter's generation may see the germ of truth in Phyllis McGinley's biting quatrain: "Snugly upon the equal heights / Enthroned at last where she belongs, / She takes no pleasure in her Rights / Who so enjoyed her wrongs."*

LIBRARY OF CONGRESS, BAIN COLLECTION

LIBRARY OF CONGRESS, FRANCES BENJAMIN JOHNSTON COLLECTION

If a white woman's place was difficult, that of the Negro woman was in most cases nearly intolerable. Yet here and there a beacon of hope appeared, and certainly none shone more brightly than the famous school at Tuskegee, Alabama, which the remarkable Booker T. Washington launched in 1881 to educate his fellow Negroes. He got white people to finance it, men like Andrew Carnegie, John D. Rockefeller, and Collis P. Huntington; he even got a small annual appropriation from the Alabama legislature. He taught his young men and women English, philosophy, and the sciences, but he also trained them in practical skills—the girls at left are learning upholstering and mattress-making, trades that they could pass on to other Negroes in their home communities. The picture comes from a superb set taken by Frances Benjamin Johnston in 1902. Twenty-one years before, Washington had started out with a handful of students, $2,000 in cash, and a tract of worn-out land. When Miss Johnston made her visit the enrollment had grown to 1,550, and the property—now boasting many buildings, some of them built by the students themselves—was worth $300,000. As a study in contrast, contemplate now another scene from the same year, taken in Chicago. It was a benefit at The Auditorium, and the nymphs, from left, are Mrs. Harry Gordon Selfridge, Mrs. Charles L. Strobel, Mrs. Joseph G. Coleman, Mrs. Samuel Insull, Mrs. Secor Cunningham, and Mrs. George Henry High. The names of the Tuskegee girls are unknown; sadly, as the poet said, the annals of the poor are short.

CHICAGO HISTORICAL SOCIETY

THE BYRON COLLECTION, MUSEUM OF THE CITY OF NEW YORK

Once upon a time a number of earnest people—bankers, for instance, and railroad presidents—thought that true ladies, when they ventured out of the home, would prefer not to associate any more than was necessary with men. The latter, of course, were great vulgar creatures who smelt of cigars and bay rum and could not always be trusted to avert their eyes when a gentlewoman inadvertently exposed her ankle. No one had explained to these officials that most inadvertence of this kind is quite advertent, and so it is to a rather strange conceit that we owe the two entertaining views on these pages, the one on the left taken by the well-known Byron Company in the special ladies' section of the New Amsterdam National Bank in 1906, the one below in the women-only car of a Hudson-Manhattan tube train in 1909. This underground railroad, which had driven its tunnel under the river Hudson only the year before, soon found that special cars for ladies were not a success and gave the idea up at the start of World War I. Yet a dogged management (how railroads live in the past!) revived the idea as recently as 1958, painting certain cars pink and banning men from them. The idea was quickly abandoned after loud cries of indignation from male passengers. Chivalry, of course, is not the only casualty of modern times; so is any desire ladies may have had for segregation. They are everywhere now, from the men's clubs to the bars, from the offices to the barbershops. The banks are all glass, exposing not only the large bills but the tellers' knees (they are girls, naturally), and the sexes fight it out for any seat that happens to be free on the train.

CULVER PICTURES

All of the medieval-looking foundation garments photographed by Isaac Taber in the advertisement below—for Mrs. W. P. Rutherford's corsets, braces, and supporters—had disappeared, along with the bustle, before the turn of the century. The well-dressed woman, between 1900 and World War I, adopted the Edwardian look, achieved with a straight-front corset that pushed the bosom up, the stomach in, and the derrière out. Since this steel-and-bone contraption could not be put on without help, it was only natural that Mrs. George Jay Gould, the mother of the children seen out automobiling on pages 314-315, posed with her lady's maid when Theodore C. Marceau photographed her at her toilet in 1908. While the mistress watches the maid put the final touches to her hair, the maid keeps a keen eye on that pearl necklace, which cost Mr. Gould half a million dollars.

BANCROFT LIBRARY

Copyright 1908
by Theo. C. Marceau. N.Y.

Byron N.Y.
7958

Separate facilities notwithstanding, nothing could check the sexual revolution that would first unmask Victorian ambivalence and then, during the First World War, smash it. Publicly this battle was joined at the point where society, by its tolerance, set its standards of taste—the theatre. In 1900 the main topic of conversation was stately Olga Nethersole, left, director and leading lady of a four-act shocker called Sapho. *Eventually Miss Nethersole found herself on trial for appearing in an indecent play; her subsequent acquittal speaks more for the changing attitudes of the day than it does for the history of drama. The play has not survived. It was a member of the Byron Company who put Olga on the pedestal prop. That same year witnessed the advent of the enormously popular Floradora Sextette. A few years later, one of these well-structured dancers caught the eye of Stanford White, and Evelyn Nesbit, shown at right in a photograph by Rudolf Eickemeyer, Jr., was soon cavorting* au naturel *on a red velvet swing in his apartment. The very thought of this and other escapades, real or imagined, later drove her millionaire husband Harry K. Thaw to pump three bullets into White's head on June 25, 1906, as the famous architect sat on the Madison Square Garden Roof listening to a performer sing "I Could Love a Million Girls." After two sensational but inconclusive murder trials, Harry Thaw was declared insane; he and Miss Nesbit were divorced in 1916, and she set about converting the scandal into a show-business career. The world was not very kind to this swinging nymph, and before her death in 1967 she said plaintively, "Stanny White was killed but my fate was worse. I lived."*

LIBRARY OF CONGRESS

HISTORY OF PHOTOGRAPHY COLLECTION, SMITHSONIAN INSTITUTION

ALL: CULVER PICTURES

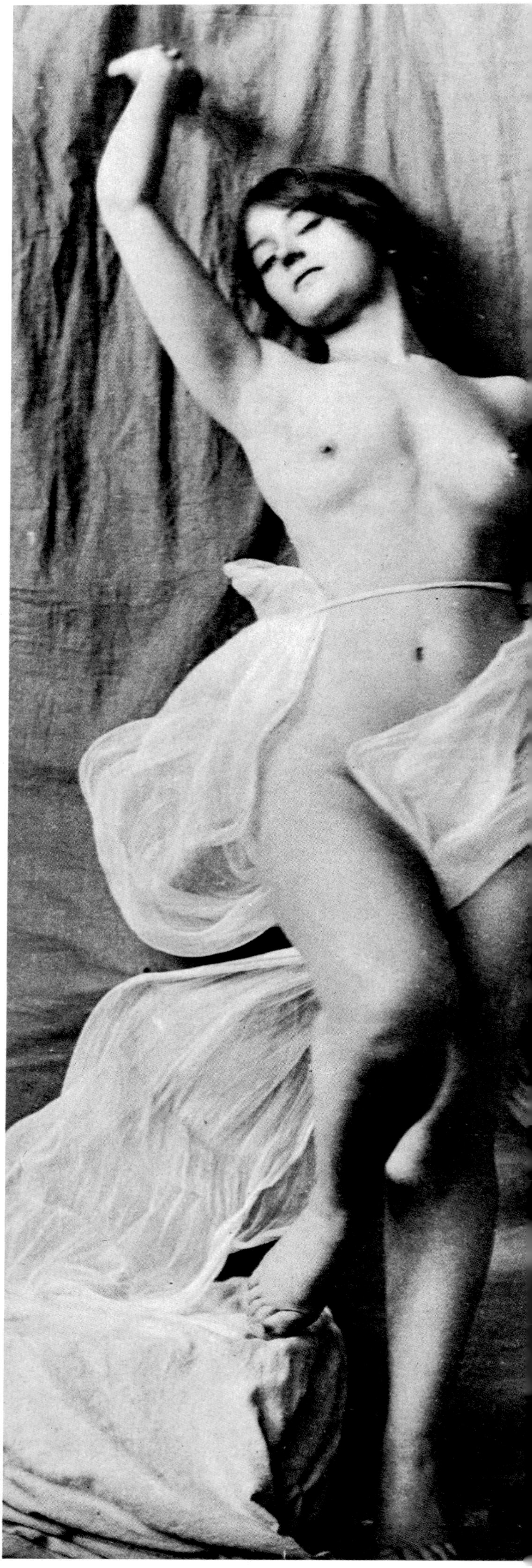

What could be more fitting for photography to focus on than the human form? Nothing, Charles Schenk of New York decided, and in 1899 he copyrighted and published some four hundred pictures which in a German edition he described as artistic nude studies, but which in English he prudently

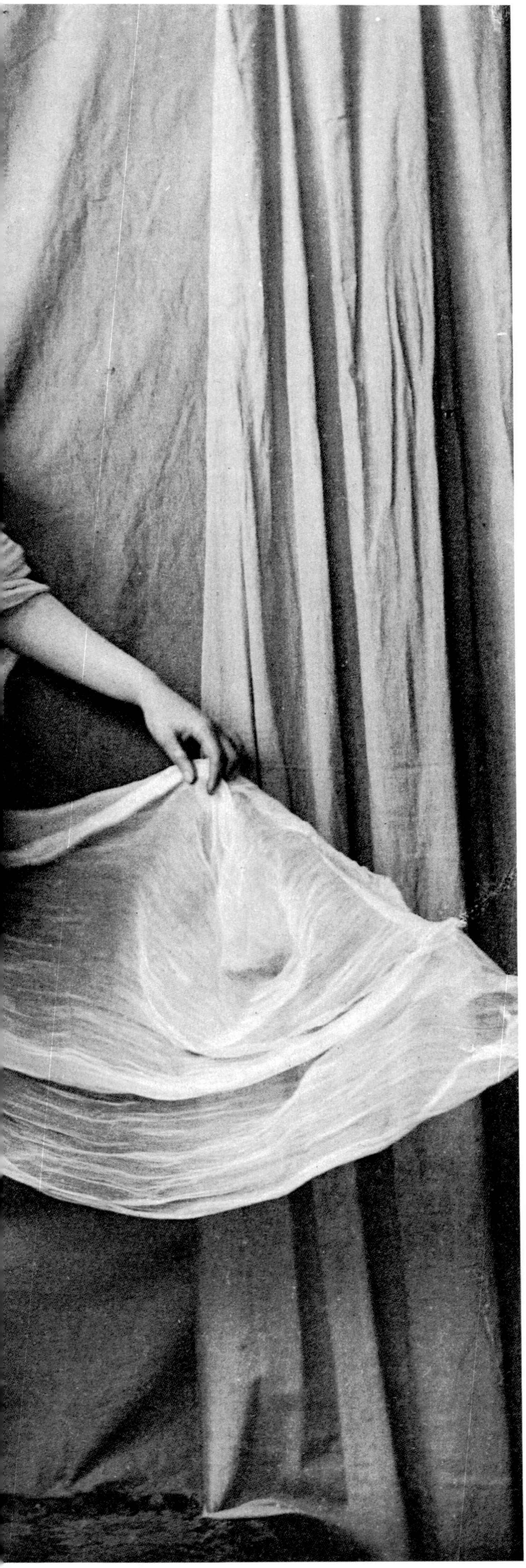

called Draperies in Action. *Here we have what is called "art photography," most earnestly undertaken, although it seems only ridiculous to modern eyes, as documentary pictures never do. The mystery is, how did Schenk manage to get the drapes to remain so delicately in place? With glue?*

The Whore with the Heart of Gold is not entirely a stylized myth of television Westerns. She existed, all right; one such soiled dove, known only as Silver Heels, performed so heroically after her more timid sisters had fled during a smallpox epidemic that the grateful miners actually named a Colorado mountain after her. The prostitute, of course, was the first woman to pursue the fortune-seeker into the wilderness, and paradoxical as it seems, she did more to tame the West than a hundred marshals. For one thing, she got the miners and ranchers and traders to bathe, if only during their periodic jaunts into town. She also imported the only culture and refinement to be found west of St. Louis, even though, as in the case of the hesitant Jezebel at right, her bureau was often better covered than she was. The most elaborate and civilized arrangements were in the more exclusive "parlor houses" like the one below, occupied by Bob Ford's girls in Creede, Colorado, during that silver town's brief glory days in the early 1890's. Who, indeed, could forget that flowery Gramophone?

COLLECTION OF FRED AND JO MAZZULLA

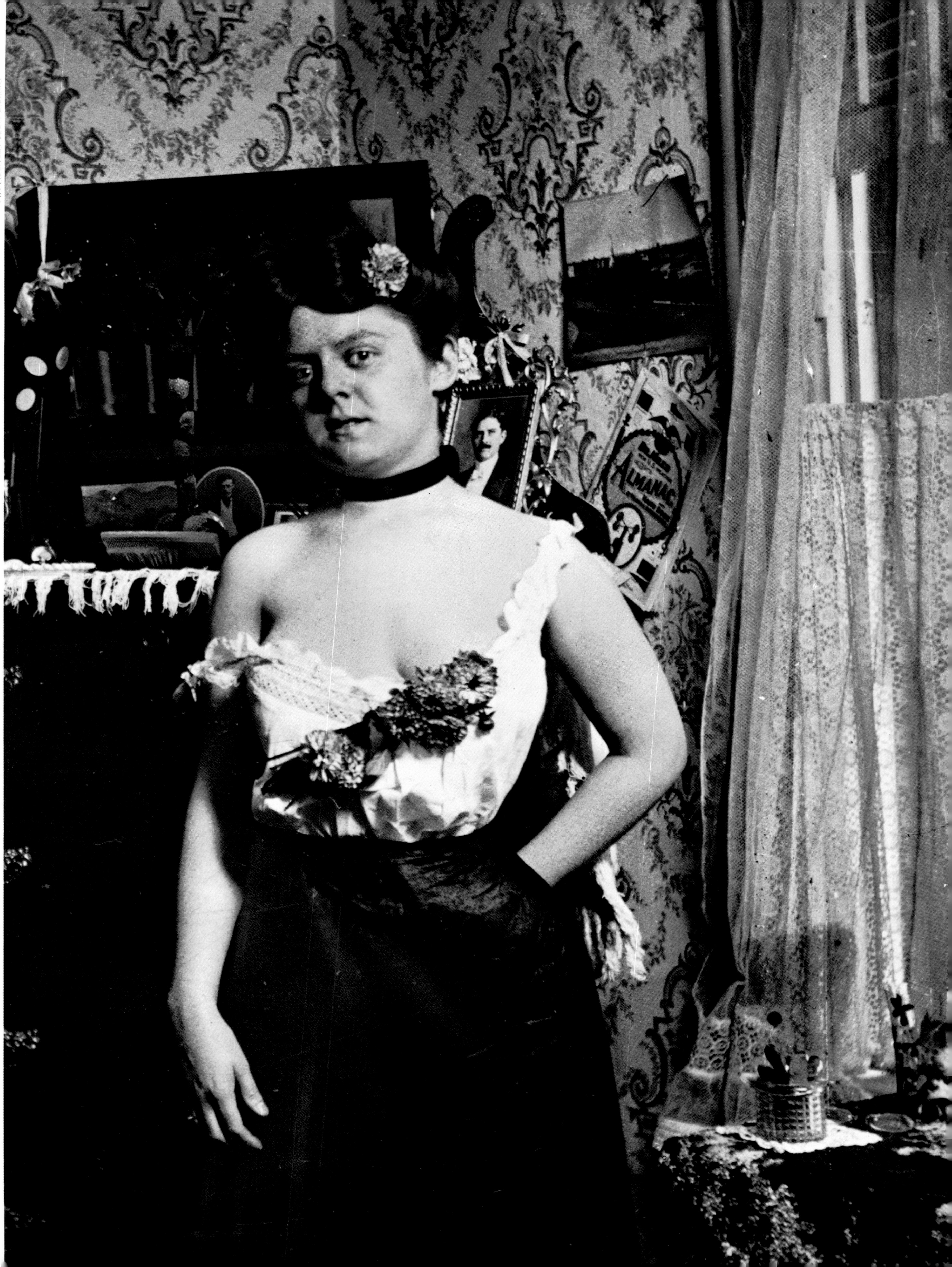

PROVIDENCE PUBLIC LIBRARY

CULVER PICTURES

A Child's Memory

Whoever said that memory enriches life but forgetfulness makes it possible must have been thinking about his or her childhood, that stolen moment in time before the advent of doubt, when we lived and died and lived again all at once, laughed and cried in a single breath, and raced barefoot, without shame, across an uneven field to stop the sun. The child sums up mankind. All our strengths and failings, our soaring aspirations and niggling jealousies, loathsome passions and tender sympathies; every emotion and impulse finds constant expression in the child. Little wonder, then, that children are continually compelling subjects for the camera. Not that the photographic image can capture the essence of this bittersweet moment, for childhood is nothing less than irresistible growth, perpetual motion, innocence unbound. What the camera does do, and in the right hands does well, is to sample the many moods of youth, to lay bare the guileless affection, to freeze momentarily the unguarded wonder. Consider, for example, this marvelous tableau that Chansonetta Emmons encountered one timeless afternoon in Kingfield, Maine. Every town, hamlet, and city, it would seem, had its own ever-changing version of Our Gang, and every boy and every girl has at one time or another been a member. Remember?

It may not have been the first building erected in town and it was usually not the grandest, but the local schoolhouse, East and West, North and South, was invariably a source of community pride. Universal education: that was the foundation of the great American dream, established by the earliest settlers and inculcated in their lineal descendants, the pioneers. Everywhere they went, anyplace they drove down roots, they began planning a school. Usually it started with a few children being tutored in someone's house by a neighborhood girl who could be spared from her domestic chores. Then a group of parents would pool their resources to outfit a small one-room shack, and perhaps even import a better-trained teacher. Finally the rest of the area would join, a school district would be formed, and the collective expression of that community's reverence for knowledge would slowly be built—stone by stone, brick by brick, log by log. Who can forget the poignant moment when the school bell first tolled for him?

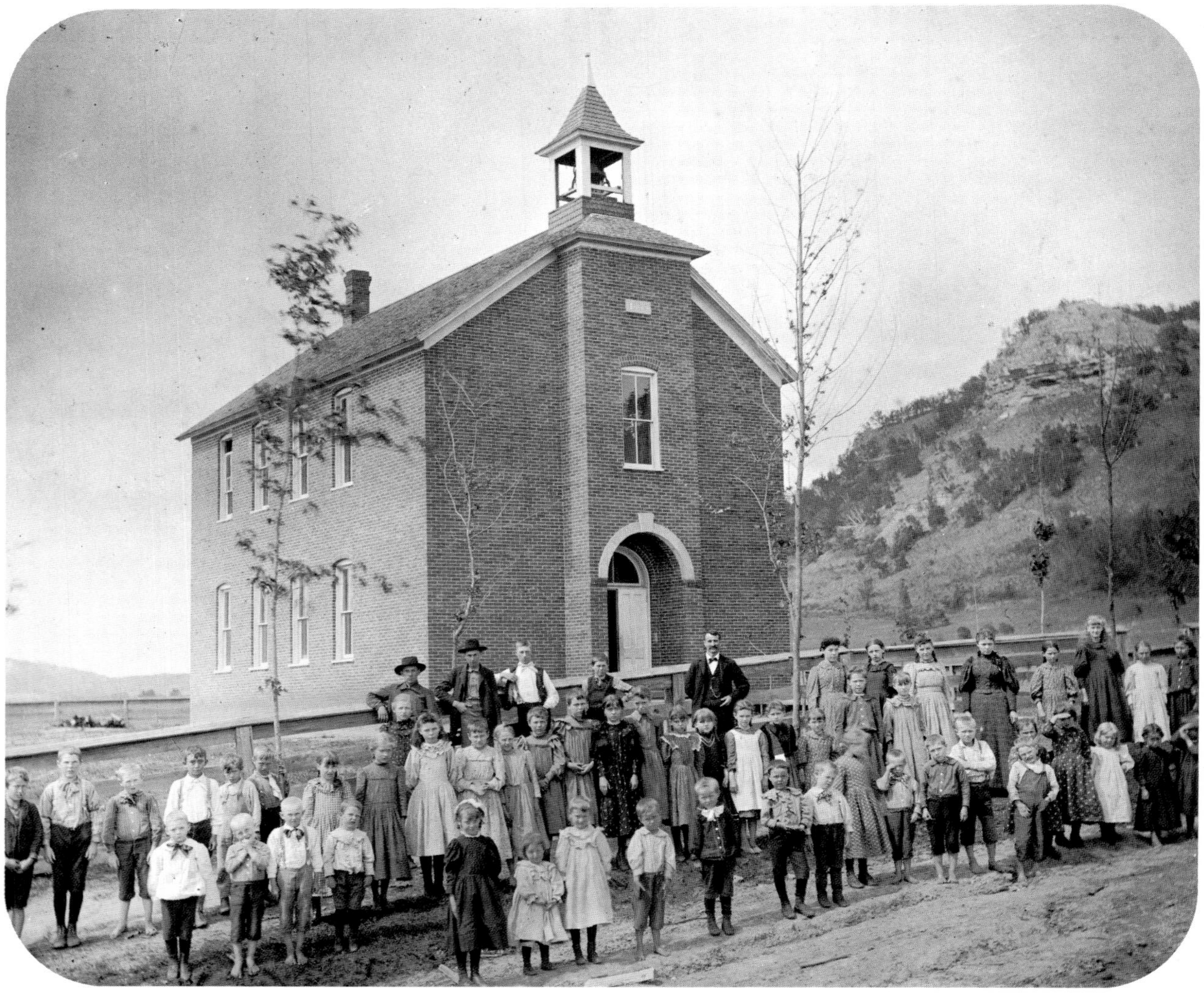

STATE HISTORICAL SOCIETY OF WISCONSIN

Alma, Wisconsin

TITLE INSURANCE AND TRUST COMPANY, LOS ANGELES

Artesia, California

STATE HISTORICAL SOCIETY OF WISCONSIN

Black River Falls, Wisconsin

LIBRARY OF CONGRESS

Helena, Montana

In his autobiography, William Allen White memorably described his first day of school: "What a day! Ma started to take me, but Pa objected. He always objected when she coddled me. Of course I liked to be coddled, and I sided with her; but he had his way. The compromise was that he said, 'I'll take him!' And so we started out. She was in the doorway, and I left her with her eyes full of tears, for she knew, having taught school, that I would never come back her baby! She knew that I was gone out of her life as a child and would return that noon a middle-aged young person, out in the world for good and all. Pa took me two blocks on my way to the schoolhouse, still three blocks away, and when he was out of sight of Ma and the doorway he prodded me with his cane in pride and affection and said: 'Now, Willie, you are a man. Go to school!' and turned and left me. He could not bear the shame of bringing me into the schoolroom, shame for him and shame for me, and we both knew it. And I trudged on . . ."

LIBRARY OF CONGRESS, CURRIER COLLECTION

Charles Currier's camera caught much of the studied informality of prep school life in this interior view, circa 1900, of Milton Academy's upper class hitting the books in the new assembly room of what is today known as Wigglesworth Hall. Seated along the rear wall are the masters charged with turning these young men into scholars. Gentlemen they were presumed to be at matriculation, and their parents were instructed to provide them with a complete wardrobe, plus a name-engraved napkin ring. Even then tuition fees were ever on the increase—in 1902 by $100, to $740.

These two young Oregon schoolgirls, caught in mid-whisper fifty-six years ago, are very likely discussing the visitor with the camera, one Roy Andrews, the district school supervisor. Andrews, in turn, was undoubtedly attracted to an obvious incongruity of rural education: these rudely clad youngsters lunching from a lard pail and cut-plug carton against a background of rather rigorous intellectual discipline.*

ANDREWS COLLECTION, UNIVERSITY OF OREGON LIBRARY

THE BETTMANN ARCHIVE

Huck Finn would have lit out for the territory before he'd have endured this kind of ordeal—just as some of these Oregon children with unnaturally clean faces probably did after W. A. Raymond got through making this garden-party picture, about 1900. After the ice cream was gone, of course.

CULVER PICTURES

Children who had everything were no problem for George Jay Gould (whose wife, Edith, is shown on *page 299**). He merely gave them imported French voiturettes, run by single-cylinder gasoline en-*

gines, then a common sight on the streets of Paris. Emulating the chauffeur at the controls of the family's nobby 1902 Panhard-Levassor were, from left, Kingdon, Marjorie, Edith, Jay, and Vivian Gould.

ALL: COLLECTION OF MARGERY HOFFMAN SMITH

ten

Parents used to chart the growth of their children with pencil marks on the alcove wall. One of the first to grasp the advantages of photographing a visual record of the trip from infancy to adulthood was Julia E. Hoffman, who posed her children annually from 1888 to 1908. "I will say," wrote her daughter Margery (shown in these pictures between ages six and sixteen), who is today Mrs. Ferdinand Smith of San Francisco, "that when we as children saw the box with accordion sides, the tripod and black cloth come out, we ducked for cover and were hard to find." Some of this adolescent annoyance comes through in a few of the pictures; by and large they form a charming series.

six

seven

eight

nine

twelve

thirteen

fourteen

fifteen

sixteen

The Pursuit of Happiness

The slogans of the new country, or, to be more precise, the "unalienable rights" it thought worth fighting for, were "Life, Liberty and the pursuit of Happiness," but we have never been very sure about the meaning of the last of these goals. In fact, the generations which came before and after the genial deistic philosophers who wrote the Declaration of Independence were very dubious about happiness. To the Puritans the pursuit of it would have smacked of traffic with the evil one and, at the very least, of what they called "mispense of time." In the nineteenth century Puritanism was back again, garbed in the dreary black vestments of the Victorian age and suspicious that happiness was something to be equated with laziness, waste, and impropriety. There was in it the bias of a lower class against a higher one, a bias which naturally extended to the amusements and pleasures of the rich as well as to their more comfortable religion. Anyone who thinks that Puritanism is dead may reflect that to this day we refer to "the problem of leisure," a phenomenon that some societies might welcome.

When the camera appeared on the scene, Victorian ideals held full sway; the New York *Herald* was attacking the "indecency" of the polka, and a seashore mob set upon a New Jersey lady who ventured to go swimming in a bathing suit. Ladies took no exercise except croquet, at which they were expected to cheat a little, and ice skating, during which they were urged to cling to the coattails of men to avoid fatigue. The lower orders, of course, indulged in a certain amount of rough sports, watched cockfights, and drank prodigiously, but all this was for some time outside the range of photography.

We are, however, an ingenious people, and we learned to enjoy ourselves thoroughly by giving pleasure other names. We called it religion, and took the steamboat to the camp meetings on Martha's Vineyard. We called it restoring our health, and headed for the clear air of the Catskills or the healing waters of Saratoga or Hot Sulphur Springs. We called it educational, a very powerful word, or "improving travel," and off we went with trunk or picnic basket. The great summer gatherings of seekers after knowledge at Chatauqua typify such pleasures; they were uplifting and fun both at once.

In time we began to develop a certain amount of common sense about exercise and plain recreation. Oliver Wendell Holmes at mid-century found the Eastern middle class "soft-muscled" and "paste-complexioned," but the rise of sports and outdoor life after the Civil War gradually ended that. According to their means and inclinations, American men took to spectator sports, to boating, hunting, fishing, water sports, and to games like tennis and golf that were unknown to them only a few decades before. In the period our book covers, we must admit, most women did not get very far beyond croquet, genteel cycling, gentle tennis, and a little dip in the water. The extensive alterations in their costume and physique would come after the First World War.

There was a class background also to the rise of leisure. The annual vacation was a rare thing in the last century and the five-day week unknown a generation or two ago. The urban poor took to parks and Sunday excursions, they flocked to circuses, parades, and games. They filled theatres, which gradually grew respectable as the century wore on. It was the well-to-do—we refrain from saying idle—who cruised, travelled, and created, by their patronage, the resort business. And it was not long before these places and their great rambling summer palaces, carefully recorded in souvenir sets of stereo slides, stopped emphasizing their appeal to the pious and the seekers of cures, for there were cards, and racing, and dancing, and flirtations, and all kinds of devilment to fill the happy hours. Here, for example, is a fragment from an 1868 travel guide, on activities in Saratoga: "For a lady: rise and dress; go down to the spring; drink to the music of the band; walk round the park; bow to gentlemen and chat a little; drink again; breakfast; see who comes in on the train; take a siesta; walk in the parlors; bow to gentlemen; have a little small-talk with gentlemen; have some gossip with ladies; dress for dinner; take dinner, an hour and a half; sit in the grounds and hear the music of the band; ride to the lake; see who comes by the evening train; dress for tea; get tea; dress for the hop; attend the hop; chat awhile in the parlors and listen to a song from some guest; go to bed. . . ."

Time for bed indeed!

PROVIDENCE PUBLIC LIBRARY

Half the business of a good time is simply going somewhere else, and it was never a more entertaining affair than at the turn of the century. The excursionists opposite are walking down to an old paddle-wheeler which will take them from Oak Bluffs, known as "the Cottage City of America," on Martha's Vineyard, to Gay Head at the other end of the island, or possibly to nearby Nantucket. Oak Bluffs was a gathering place for Methodists as well as more secular visitors, and one could put up at the Naumkeag, Pawnee, or Wesley hostelries for $2.50 to $3.50 a day. Gay Head, the object of the daytime and moonlight excursions, was described by Karl Baedeker, a slavish Anglophile, as very much like Alum Bay on the Isle of Wight. Praise indeed. You could go inspect the powerful lighthouse beacon and ride an omnibus driven by a genuine, or fairly genuine, native Indian. Some people, of course, prefer mountains, and those the Catskills offered in profusion. The steep slopes were dotted with picturesque inns—inexpensive at $1 to $3 a day, and easy to reach via such summer-only lines as the Kaaterskill Railway (below) which took you to the famous Catskill Mountain House. All these railways have vanished, as have the picturesque stagecoaches that met them from remote points.

LIBRARY OF CONGRESS

The four pleasant scenes on these two pages show a little of what awaited the well-heeled vacationer of a century ago when he finally completed his journey. They are taken from stereoscopic views of the period 1868-1878. At right, in a photograph by Seneca R. Stoddard of Glens Falls, New York, a coach arrives with its affluent cargo at the Fort William Henry Hotel at Lake George. Ten years later the rates were $17.50 to $28 per week, a fast-running elevator had been installed, and the hotel thoughtfully provided hourly stock-market bulletins.

"From the waterfall he named her, / Minnehaha, Laughing Water." Here is the gleeful cataract itself, dropping Minnehaha Creek ninety-three feet as it rushes toward the nearby Mississippi. These vacationers, in a stereo by Charles A. Zimmerman of St. Paul, Minnesota, may have come because of Longfellow's Hiawatha*—most people did. As for the poet, he never saw the falls; his inspiration apparently came from a daguerreotype, made in 1852 by one Alexander Hesler of Chicago, that somehow found its way to his home in Cambridge, Massachusetts.*

These gentlefolk, whether pure hedonists or victims of digestive disorders, are gathered by a veritable jewel of a drinking fountain in Congress Park, at Saratoga Springs, New York. Whether for its healing waters (which were carbonated and so cathartic that they were variously categorized as "walking" or "running"), or for its famous racecourse, Saratoga attracted a large and elegant patronage, running heavily to wealthy old sports and young consorts of amazing beauty and doubtful antecedents. The stereo is by Baker and Record, who served the souvenir trade.

The most memorable place in Saratoga, also immortalized by Baker and Record, was the porch of your resort hotel, where everybody met, gossiped, flirted, settled wagers, listened to concerts, and rested up for the racing, the dancing, and the titanic dinners—which ran to eight courses, lasted two hours, and kept the local death rate satisfactorily stable. The scene at left is the inner court of the famous Grand Union, which covered seven acres of land, had one solid mile of piazzas, and seated fourteen hundred at dinner, attended by two hundred and fifty waiters.

ALL: AMERICAN HERITAGE COLLECTION

COLLECTION OF DICK LEMEN

The good-natured couple perched delicately on lily pads, which was a favorite photographic pastime of the day, were probably taken by Charles C. Clement. They are in St. Louis' Tower Grove Park, once a popular spot for picnics, dances, and sports, and the giant water lilies were grown from Amazon

River seeds. The park's benefactor, Henry Shaw, a real-estate tycoon turned somewhat-overzealous-horticulturist, obviously prized the pads more than the perchers. For their protection, the lilies were covered by blankets and weight-distributing frames, and were approached on wooden walkways.

Pueblo, Colorado, July 4, 1905: Here in an early action shot is the afternoon plunge of Eunice Winkless, a daring amateur who, said the local paper, clung "to the mane as the horse dived headlong . . . to the pool of water below" and "emerged dripping" (how else?) to claim her prize of $100.

STANFORD UNIVERSITY ARCHIVES

What today's onlooker might regard as a modern sculpture is actually a mound of bonfire components for a 1910 football rally at Stanford University. For whatever reason—rampant pyromania or surplus combustibles—this Stanford bonfire rally, which began by accident in 1898, became an annual event.

CULVER PICTURES

NEWPORT HISTORICAL SOCIETY

One of the most popular of all spectator sports was horse racing, though from the stalwart stances of the men gathered at Brooklyn's Gravesend track at Sheepshead Bay at left, it is hard to believe that anything in close proximity is moving. With the exception of several déclassé derbies, the going headgear seems to be the straw boater; the prevailing facial expression denotes either myopia or languor; and the accepted passion appears to have been restraint. Nonetheless, when Leonard W. Jerome, grandfather of Sir Winston Churchill, opened the Coney Island Jockey Club in 1879, he had on his hands a sure moneymaker. The Gravesend track opened in 1880; in 1885 the successful Dwyer brothers, noticing that the ownership of a racetrack seemed to be "more profitable than owning race horses," organized the popular Brooklyn Jockey Club; and 1894 saw the inauguration of the famous Aqueduct course. Although this photograph would lead one to assume that the predominant sex in attendance was male, the sport also captivated women, who flocked around the grandstands and clubhouses, most of which offered not only a good view of the races but also such luxuries as dining rooms and balconies. On the day this photograph was taken the attendance was estimated at forty thousand, about the same as on a typical summer Saturday today. In similar spirit and dress one could, and did, observe sailboat racing. In the lower photograph, the spectators are probably watching the annual New York Yacht Club races from Castle Hill at Newport, Rhode Island. The objects of their attention, however, are not visible in the picture (the small gaff-rigged boats in the foreground are spectator craft). Begun in 1844 as a cruise, the N.Y.Y.C. event developed into an annual competition for the coveted Astor Cup.

It is obvious from Frances Benjamin Johnston's photograph below that sporting attire had not taken hold in 1905. Fortunately, the elegantly clad lady about to board a yacht in Oyster Bay, Long Island, was in all probability asked to contribute nothing more to the sail than her presence. Occasionally a woman like Mrs. C. Oliver Iselin came along, who twice in the 1890's served on the crew of America's Cup defenders, in the afterguard; but most women, and even men, boarded with expectations of merely luxuriating among all the comforts of their Park Avenue apartments or Southampton estates. The rooms may have been fewer but they were equally plush, abounding in the same ponderous draperies, gilt furniture, and oriental rugs. Not every sail could be termed an unmitigated success. An unknown photographer, having either a premonition of disaster or an exceptionally speedy camera, or both, caught the collision (opposite) of the Virginia *and the incautious* Little Annie *in San Francisco Bay sometime near the turn of the century. One hopes no elegantly attired ladies were on board the smaller* Little Annie.

OVERLEAF: *You could also sail on ice, or sand, like these sports on the smooth, hard strand at Ormond Beach, Florida. Henry M. Flagler's new Florida East Coast Railway brought thither the new breed of automobile racers, along with old folks who wished to be pedalled about on vehicles like the one seen at far right, and elderly John D. Rockefeller, the oil king, who came to visit "The Casements," his winter home.*

LIBRARY OF CONGRESS, DETROIT PUBLISHING COMPANY COLLECTION

LIBRARY OF CONGRESS, FRANCES BENJAMIN JOHNSTON COLLECTION

SAN FRANCISCO MARITIME MUSEUM

THE ADIRONDACK MUSEUM

LIBRARY OF CONGRESS

During the Victorian period, they just couldn't leave a room alone. An example of the horror vacui *which seemed to sweep the country is the Trophy Room (left) at Brandreth Lake in the Adirondacks. Benjamin Brandreth, founder of the family that still owns the area, began his career making Brandreth's Universal Vegetable Pills. He must have seized on some universal deficiency, for wealth pouring in from the business enabled him in 1851 to purchase twenty-five thousand acres in the Adirondacks. Hunting had become a sport of great prestige, and trophy collecting (either by hunt or mere purchase) a popular hobby. Fox hunting had been called "the sport of kings, the image of war without its guilt, and only five-and-twenty per cent of its danger," and duck shooting shared the honors. Judging from the photograph above, taken by Seneca R. Stoddard in 1891, the sport required little energy; its major risk was perhaps defined in a story in an 1882* Harper's Weekly *of a duck shooter "driven mad from listening year after year to the same stories told over and over again by his partner."*

The Wisconsin Dells, at left, were described in the nineteenth century as "a wondrous, witch-like tangle of cliffs, crags, caverns and gulches, of strange-shaped towering rocks, yawning chasms and roaring floods." The area was developed, largely through the talents of photographer Henry Hamilton Bennett, into a thriving tourist attraction. Returning there after the Civil War, Bennett quickly tired of the standard portraiture of the day; leaving that part of his business to his wife, he spent his hours exploring the Dells and capturing their uniqueness in three-dimensional pictures. Using the unwieldy photographic equipment of the day, he managed, by moistening his plates with sponges, to make time exposures within the dark caves, and created an ingenious rubber-band-triggered "high-speed" shutter. One of the first photographers to shoot a "picture story," Bennett made a complete record of a logging trip down the treacherous Wisconsin River, even managing to capture on film several white-water adventures. Charles Currier took the picture below of a relaxed group of hunters, who were very likely taking a bachelor vacation somewhere along the New England coast.

LIBRARY OF CONGRESS, CURRIER COLLECTION

The length of the skis below, photographed in Colorado in 1897, and of the bathing costumes at right, which date to the mid-1880's, would convulse the crowds on any modern ski slope or beach. They would have astounded ante bellum America, too, which took as little exercise as possible, regarded snow as very nearly impassable, except on webbed snowshoes, and thought mixed bathing morally hazardous. When skis first made their appearance in this country, they were widely known as "Norwegian snowshoes," and they were as long as fourteen feet. With only toe straps and heel blocks to secure them to your feet, and a single long pole for what small help it offered, you had little control. When the group at right posed, a woman's bathing costume used ten yards of material, as compared with less than one yard in a bikini. A corset was advised, and skirts were required, even if they made the act of swimming nearly impossible. The bare arms, which were frowned on, and the faintly Bohemian air of the man at left would seem to indicate that these Newport, Rhode Island, swimmers were a raffish lot. Not a bit; the gentleman was Horatio B. Wood, amateur photographer, church organist, and a power in the Sons of Temperance.

COLLECTION OF FRED AND JO MAZZULLA

NEWPORT HISTORICAL SOCIETY

COLLECTION OF IRL G. WHITCHURCH

This affecting woodland scene should serve to remind us, amidst all the contrasts in this book, that some things change very little, especially courtship and love. Despite all the hazards, indeed roadblocks, placed in the way of romance in Victorian days, the human species seemed to carry on. Boys and girls in America always enjoyed considerably more liberty in being together than the young in Europe, a fact continually astounding to foreign visitors; the "rules," in pre-Freudian times, seem to have been self-enforcing. Before the automobile, "petting" was something that happened to the cat. Marriage was a lady's career, for, as Catharine Beecher put it, "The family state is the aptest earthly illustration of the heavenly kingdom." She was the sister of Harriet Beecher Stowe and Henry Ward Beecher, and she was never married herself. The picture here was taken in Maine by Chansonetta Emmons, and it shows her niece Blanche May Stanley with a swain named Edward M. Hallett. The young couple did marry, in 1902.

NATIONAL PARK SERVICE

GEORGE EASTMAN HOUSE COLLECTION

There are always a few ebullient people for whom showing off is a joy. On Overhanging Rock at Glacier Point in Yosemite National Park (where we showed pioneer photographer William H. Jackson, on page 58), a waitress named Kitty Tatch and a friend cavort for George Fiske, official photographer of Yosemite for almost forty years, about 1895. Kitty worked at the nearby Sentinel Hotel, and would autograph this frightening picture for the tourists. Above, an anonymous but courageous man jumps from a ledge to a pinnacle called Stand Rock in the Dells of the Wisconsin River, in a stereograph made by Henry Hamilton Bennett. It is not a long way across, but . . .

Then as now, the young had a life of their own. Clothed or unclothed, boys headed for swimming holes, creeks, and rivers, as in the scene opposite, taken by a photographer for the famous old Detroit Publishing Company. The locale is Lester Park on Lake Superior, just a little east of Duluth, Minnesota, which in those days termed itself the "Zenith City of the Unsalted Seas," and had grown from eighty white inhabitants in 1860 to some sixty-five thousand in 1905, about when this picture was taken. Girls, unlike these boys, were very proper, especially after going into long dresses. There was no frolicking in the water, even in warm Anniston, Alabama, where this school outing celebrating graduation day was immortalized in 1890, at newly opened Oxford Lake Park, by Sam Russell, a local man.

CULVER PICTURES

The clown in mankind is never far below the surface, especially since it takes such a little alteration—an overzealous hug, a little switch in headgear—to turn the normal into the ridiculous, or tragedy into comedy. Revolutionary soldiers cut up and even Puritans must have made faces on occasion, but art tells us nothing of it—only the camera, freezing the idle moment, records forgotten japes. The picture below was taken somewhere in Florida by one W. Frank Clark, around 1900-1910, and the one at right in Connecticut, about the same time.

OVERLEAF: *We take our leave of old-time America with this moody scene on the rocks at Ogunquit Pond, Maine, around 1910. The young woman is Dorothy Stanley Emmons, then about nineteen, daughter of the Mrs. Emmons whose pictures we have used so often. What her thoughts were, long ones or short, and why she stared so wistfully across the peaceful water, no one can say. That was sixty years ago, and Dorothy, like her relatively quiet and peaceful era, is dead and gone.*

CULVER PICTURES

LIBRARY OF CONGRESS

PICTURE SOURCES

The Adirondack Museum, Blue Mountain Lake, N. Y.
American Automobile Association, Washington, D.C.
American Museum of Photography, Philadelphia, Pa.
Ralph W. Andrews, Seattle, Wash.
Bancroft Library, Berkeley, Calif.
Dr. Philip Batchelder, Providence, R. I.
Beinecke Library, Yale University, New Haven, Conn.
Charles J. Belden Estate, St. Petersburg, Fla.
The Bennett Studio, Wisconsin Dells, Wis.
The Bettmann Archive, New York, N. Y.
Brown Brothers, New York, N. Y.
California Palace of the Legion of Honor, San Francisco, Calif.
Cape Cod Photos, Orleans, Mass.
Carnegie Library of Pittsburgh, Pittsburgh, Pa.
Mrs. Joseph Carson, Philadelphia, Pa.
Chicago Historical Society, Chicago, Ill.
Cincinnati Public Library, Cincinnati, Ohio
Josephine Cobb, Washington, D.C.
Culver Pictures, New York, N. Y.
Robert E. Cunningham, Stillwater, Okla.
Robert H. Dennis, Williamsburg, Va.
Denver Public Library, Denver, Colo.
Detroit Public Library, Detroit, Mich.
George Eastman House, Rochester, N. Y.
Glenbow Foundation, Calgary, Alberta, Canada
Haynes Studios Inc., Bozeman, Mont.
David Hoffman, New York, N. Y.
H. Lawrence Hoffman, Sea Cliff, N. Y.
Henry E. Huntington Library and Art Gallery, San Marino, Calif.
Dr. Joseph Johnson House, Charleston, S. C.
Daniel W. Jones, New York, N. Y.
Kansas State Historical Society, Topeka, Kans.
University of Kansas, Lawrence, Kans.
Edith LaFrancis, Agawam, Mass.
Dick Lemen, St. Louis, Mo.
Library of Congress, Washington, D. C.
Los Angeles County Museum of Natural History, Los Angeles, Calif.
Stephen D. Maguire, Belmar, N. J.
Maine Historical Society, Portland, Me.
The Massillon Museum, Massillon, Ohio
Fred and Jo Mazzulla, Denver, Colo.
Minnesota Historical Society, St. Paul, Minn.
Missouri Historical Society, St. Louis, Mo.
State Historical Society of Missouri, Columbia, Mo.
Montana Historical Society, Helena, Mont.
Museum of the City of New York, New York, N. Y.
The Museum of Modern Art, New York, N. Y.
National Archives, Washington, D.C.
National Park Service, Washington, D.C.
Nebraska State Historical Society, Lincoln, Neb.
New Haven Colony Historical Society, New Haven, Conn.
Newport Historical Society, Newport, R. I.
New York State Historical Association, Cooperstown, N. Y.
Ohio State University, Columbus, Ohio
University of Oklahoma Library, Norman, Okla.
University of Oregon Library, Eugene, Ore.
Lloyd Ostendorf, Dayton, Ohio
The Historical Society of Pennsylvania, Philadelphia, Pa.
The Polk Ancestral Home, Columbia, Tenn.
Providence Public Library, Providence, R. I.
Dr. Robert G. Reed, Fort Scott, Kans.
Rhode Island Historical Society, Providence, R. I.
Dick Rudisill, Boulder City, Nev.
The San Francisco Maritime Museum, San Francisco, Calif.
Seattle Public Library, Seattle, Wash.
Margery Hoffman Smith, San Francisco, Calif.
Smithsonian Institution, Washington, D.C.
Society for the Preservation of New England Antiquities, Boston, Mass.
Andrew Spano, Yorktown Heights, N. Y.
Stanford University Archives, Stanford, Calif.
Staten Island Historical Society, Staten Island, N. Y.
Sterling Memorial Library, Yale University, New Haven, Conn.
Sutter's Fort State Historical Monument, Sacramento, Calif.
Pauline Dakin Taft, Coconut Grove, Fla.
Time-Out Antiques, New York, N. Y.
Title Insurance and Trust Co., Los Angeles, Calif.
United States Geological Survey, Washington, D.C.
Utah State Historical Society, Salt Lake City, Utah
The Valentine Museum, Richmond, Va.
Robert A. Weinstein, Los Angeles, Calif.
Wells Fargo Bank History Room, San Francisco, Calif.
Whaling Museum and Old Dartmouth Historical Society, New Bedford, Mass.
Irl G. Whitchurch, Wheat Ridge, Colo.
State Historical Society of Wisconsin, Madison, Wis.

Acknowledgments

Whatever merit this book may have lies in its use of photographs not widely known or previously published. The authors passed over many outstanding but familiar pictures by America's great photographers of our early years in order to uncover fresh ones which we felt were equally compelling. Our efforts in this direction led us, therefore, to many rich and varied collections, private and public, whose resources would easily furnish the materials for a dozen more books.

No listing of the places from which came the final collection of photographs shown here can indicate how many other institutions and private individuals have generously opened their photographic files to us during the growth of this book. The selection was a highly personal one on the part of the book's three authors, and it necessarily meant discarding many favorites.

Many of these collections we visited and browsed through happily in person. But since the hundreds of historical societies in North America are too scattered to permit a separate investigation in each, we sent out a letter of inquiry. Its subsequent publication in *History News,* the newsletter of the American Association of State and Local History, resulted in some fine contributions by alert picture librarians, for which we are most grateful. If pictures from the State Historical Society of Wisconsin and the Chicago Historical Society appear often in these pages, it is in large part thanks to Paul Vanderbilt and Mrs. Mary Frances Rhymer, whose knowledge and taste are widely respected.

Over the years AMERICAN HERITAGE magazine has made extensive use of the extraordinarily rich files of the Library of Congress, the National Archives, and the Smithsonian Institution. For this book, with the help of their experienced and competent staffs, we delved into their special collections with highly rewarding results. In particular, we would like to thank Miss Virginia Daiker of the Library of Congress, whose aid and encouragement to us over the years has been of inestimable value.

The pictures from the museums, great libraries, and university collections included in this book represent only a fraction of what we know to be available in archives all over the country. We were distressed not to have been able to visit all of them. Two university collections seem to us to be especially worthy of mention. The first of these is housed at the University of Kansas, where the late Robert Taft carefully assembled the glass plates of photographer Joseph J. Pennell, and it offers a remarkable look at Junction City and Fort Riley, Kansas, in the years 1895-1909. The second is at the University of Oklahoma, where an outstanding western history collection is ably directed by Jack Haley.

To the many private collectors, both those whose names appear at the left and the countless others whose pictures could not be included, we owe a special vote of thanks. Many of our most delightful hours have been spent with them, sharing their enthusiasms and drawing on their knowledge.

Again, in particular we would like to single out two individuals whose contributions to this book cannot be adequately measured. Each one is a connoisseur and, more important, a lover of these old photographs, and in their generosity they have led us to many sources, as well as opening their own files to us. To Daniel W. Jones of Project 20 of the National Broadcasting Company, which does so many brilliant television programs using old pictures, and to Robert A. Weinstein of the Ward Ritchie Press, Graphics Editor of *The American West* and consultant to many western museums, we are profoundly grateful.

We have been kindly assisted by many members of the staff of AMERICAN HERITAGE, both those listed on the contents page and others who are not. As to the latter, we should like particularly to express our appreciation to Robert Reynolds, Managing Editor of AMERICAN HERITAGE; Brenda Niemand, Copy Editor; Robert Gallagher, Associate Editor; the staff of the American Heritage book division; and the production department of this company.

The final acknowledgment of this book must sadly take the form of a memorial. The death of our great friend, D. Jay Culver, at the very moment this book was going to press, brought into focus his great contribution to all picture books during the forty-two years since Culver Pictures opened its doors. His keen eye, his fund of knowledge, his wit, his sheer delight in the world of old pictures, will be missed by all of us.

MALT EXTRACT
The Best Tonic
CHESTER BEER
A. Van Beuren & Co.
GIVES VIM BOUNCE.
IT BRACES.
OLUMBIA
UP
BALL
UNITED
UNION
CLARENDON HALL
BALL
UNITED
UNION
CLARENDON HALL